AF268779

52 weeks of horror

Prompts and inspiration
by Halfplanet Press

Other books by
HALFPLANET PRESS

SCIENCE FICTION
Who Built The Humans?
The Stephanie Glitch

POETRY
False Vacuum
Branch Density

FANTASY / YA
Of Shadows, Demons, and Lost Brothers

COMING SOON
52 weeks of Science Fiction
52 weeks of Comedy
52 weeks of Poetry

52 weeks of horror

Halfplanet Press

This book belongs to

____

Their favourite genre is

____

Introduction

This isn't an ordinary prompt book. This is a book that challenges you to reflect on your progress after writing, to conceptualise the physical shape of your story, to seek previously unseen areas for improvement, and to remember inspirational moments on your journey as a writer. The goal is that at the end of the next year, you will know more about yourself, and will have refined your talents and experimented with types of writing you might not have considered otherwise. Basically, this book will cause you to mutate into a better writer.

For this book I created a list of deceptively simple and piercing questions that will not only give you a deeper insight into your own writing processes, but that will inspire you to continue to find more insights in the future. These questions are inspired by my work running a Creative Writing society, and from my experience on a Creative Writing Master's degree. My mum told me to brag about that. Hi mum.

I settled on 52 prompts because one a week should be a manageable goal for most writers. This way you can put more effort into each prompt, and get more creative sustenance out of it than you would have done managing a larger quantity of smaller projects. For this reason the prompts are written in a way that encourages detailed storytelling, and each comes with a set of reflective questions and space for planning. There are also additional activities at the end of each 4 week block, allowing you to chart your progress as a writer over time. You can use this data to plot your trajectory, and work out where you think you might be going. This method works for me, and I believe it will work for you too.

Now you have this book in your hands, you are a student. Your teacher is your future self. Make them proud.

Stay innovative.
- Halfplanet Press

Motivation

1. Accept that you are human and need breaks sometimes. You might not have writer's block, you might just have drink block or adventure block. Go get a drink, have an adventure, then return to your project.

2. These days a lot of people say should always accept yourself, that you are always perfect as you are. Unfortunately some other people make the very good point that this can lead to complacency, to artist's giving up on progress because they aren't motivated to improve. You will probably be switching between these two ideas at different times of the day, so I'd like to offer a compromise. Repeat the following to yourself. "I am okay as I am today, because I am working on something for tomorrow."
This means that thinking about tomorrow counts as working on yourself and your art, because tomorrow you will know what needs to be done.

3. Quite a lot of the writing process is daydreaming. You don't have to sit in a black and white room looming over a typewriter all day, you can go outside or think about your stories almost anywhere.

4. You can't always control your immediate environment. Noisy streets, unsupportive people and looming deadlines will often trick writers into thinking they have a writing block. I'll be honest with you, I don't believe writing blocks exist in the way most people imagine them, I think most of the time the blockages are external. Luckily you can sneak around these by retraining yourself. Try to find a moment of time where you can sit and think. Even if this is five minutes at the end or beginning of a day, it might be enough for that next big idea to fit in.

5. Every scene deserves a soundtrack. Find yourself something that reminds you of your project, and play it whenever you are working on it. Soon enough every time you listen to it your brain will start writing in the background, and you will find it easier to process and to remember ideas.

6. If you give each scene its own song, then you can teleport your writing brain to any point of your story with ease.

Goals

You are encouraged not just to use these prompts as strict guides, but to be inspired by them, to stray from them, and to make them weird. You should always look for ways to experiment and discover. Doing so will not only test your imagination and skills more than simply copying the base idea of the prompt, it will protect you against future awkwardness if some of you decide to share your stories.

With that in mind, let's both set some lofty goals for the next year.

My goal is to get at least six more similar books onto shelves and into your classrooms and studies, so that you can piece together a whole year where every day has a prompt, if you're brave enough.

Your goal is to

by the time you finish this book.
That's a good goal. You can do it.

How it works

In the original draft of this book I had given each prompt a shape based on its potential attributes, each ranked out of 10. These attributes were Fear, Shock, Originality, Suspense, Realism, and Action. Later in the process I realised it was much more sensible to invite you to decide upon the shape of the story yourself. So below every prompt you will find a simple graph that looks like this.

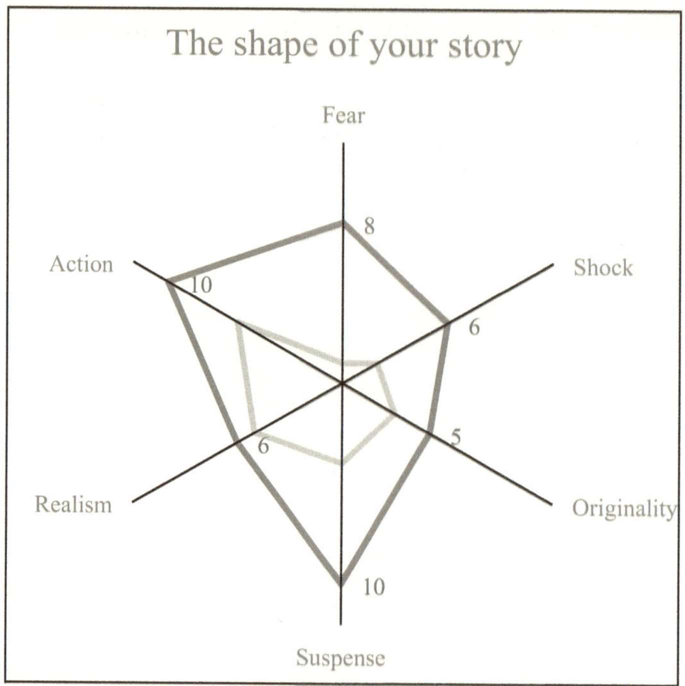

All you have to do is write your story, or imagine the story, and fill this in. It will help you translate your story from that weird amorphous thing in your head to something almost tangible on paper. That way you can see which bits need work, which bits you might want to trim or add to. I always see stories as shapes, and it helps me know where I am going with them. You can also use these story shapes as additional prompts in the future, by trying to write a story with the same prompt, but the opposite shape. You could experiment and see what a story with high shock and low action would be like.

The shape of your story

Fear

is the amount of audience/character fear generated overall. If you're going for lighter horror or even horror comedy, this will typically be a low number, but it doesn't have to be.

Shock

is defined not only as shocking or jumpscare moments, but those moments where a reader does not expect the next twist.

Originality

is how far away your work is from other known work. It's impossible to have an entirely original thought (and if you did nobody would understand it) so this can be measured as how well you make an idea your own. Do you bring a new twist to an old type of story?

Suspense

is how tense a story gets as the audience waits for something to happen. This is closely related to fear, though it does not always generate it, as suspense can be used for comedy or for teasing twists in the plot. Stories with high realism might have more suspense as they are more plausible to the reader, and the story world will be more understandable to them, making it easier for the writer to set up the stakes.

Realism

is defined as how close to reality your story universe is. Most audiences won't know whether or not a car explodes if you shoot it a few times, so this category's rules are up to you, depending on your audience.

Action

can be defined as how physical the story gets. Are there many fights or scenes where your characters have to traverse difficult terrain? Do they run away from something? Action doesn't have to be a vital part of your story, but it's a good way to bring out the inner conflict between characters and to bring in twists to the plot, or to derail the character's plans.

Examples for shaping

Fear

Something is out to kill your characters, and it knows the ins and outs of this abandoned military base better than they do.

Shock

The established protagonist to your story is killed off early on. The narrative then moves to a background character. This establishes with your reader that anyone can die at any moment.

Originality

If I wrote anything here it would stop being original once you used it. You get the idea. Do something that is uniquely you. Write the story that nobody else can.

Suspense

Your characters wait for the lift to take them to a safe floor. You can play this scene in multiple ways. You can subvert expectation by having nothing outside waiting for them, or something funny, or a character they thought was dead, or perhaps a murderous robot. You can also use the time in the lift for your characters to get in some quick dialogue. The lift might even break half way to its destination, forcing them onto a floor they know is dangerous.

Realism

The lift is actually flying around inside a hollowed out planet, and it is made of bones and viscera. Creepy, but it does dismantle the stakes usually associated with lifts in stories. Who knows, this lift might sprout wings at any second.

Action

Rather predictably, your cold-hearted character decides to sacrifice themselves, winning the battle against the skeleton army. The protagonist's love interest somehow has enough time during the chaos to profess their feelings for your protagonist, before knocking out a skeleton soldier without even looking. Cool.

Getting to know yourself

This is the part where you spend an agonising two minutes trying to work out who you are. Sorry about the existential crisis, it happens. Be as honest as you can, you will be referring back to this section in the future. It will be good to reflect and see if you've changed as a writer.

Name/Pen name

Favourite genres of writing

Is this different for other forms of media? If so, why?

Favourite author? (based on their writing style)

Least favourite thing writers do? (be harsh)

Something you avoid writing about (and why)

Something you love writing about.

Your goals for the next year.

1.   At an early screening for an interactive horror movie, your characters discover that they are the unwitting protagonists.

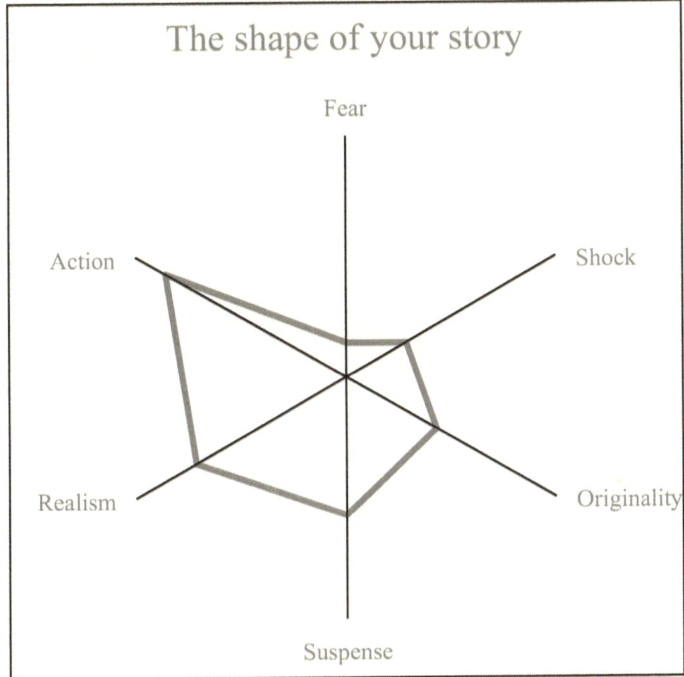

Plot outline:

Characters:

Character motives/what drives the story:

What makes this story unique to you:

2.   An old doll is found in the loft of a house. Your character throws it away, and weeks later it shows up outside her place of work. But there's one problem: nobody else can see it.

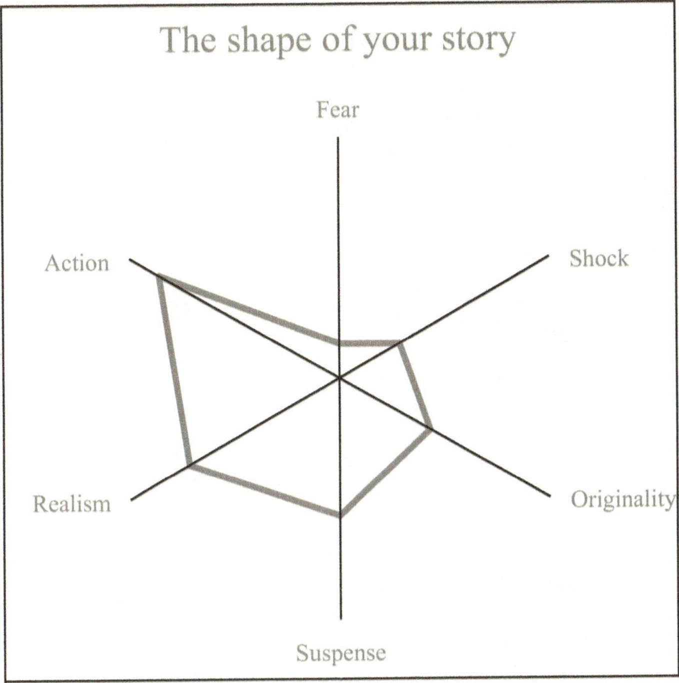

Plot outline:

Characters:

Character motives/what drives the story:

What makes this story unique to you:

3.	A body is discovered in the Himalayas. It seems to have been crushed from all sides at once, and drained of all blood.

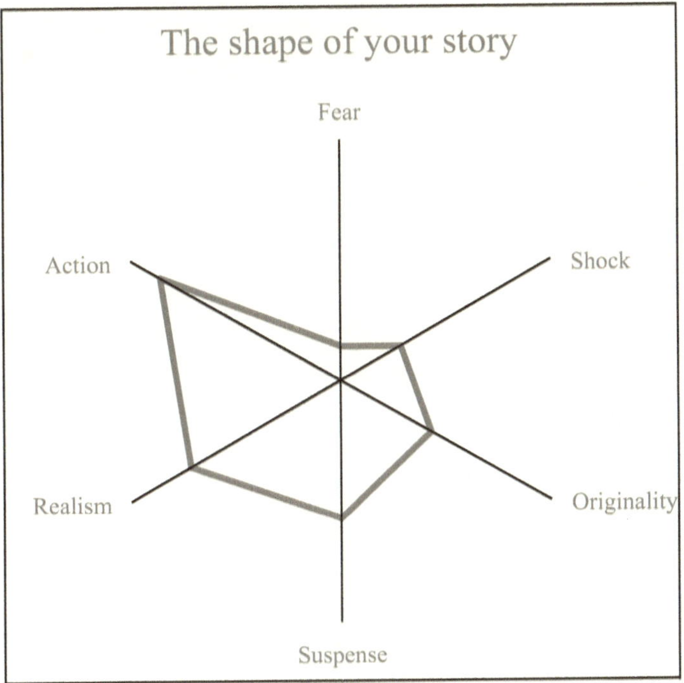

Plot outline:

Characters:

Character motives/what drives the story:

What makes this story unique to you:

4.   Radioactive mutants climb out of the lake of a rural town. The government steps in to kill them, until one of them starts talking to a soldier, remembering his face from a horrifying past life filled with brutal scientific experiments.

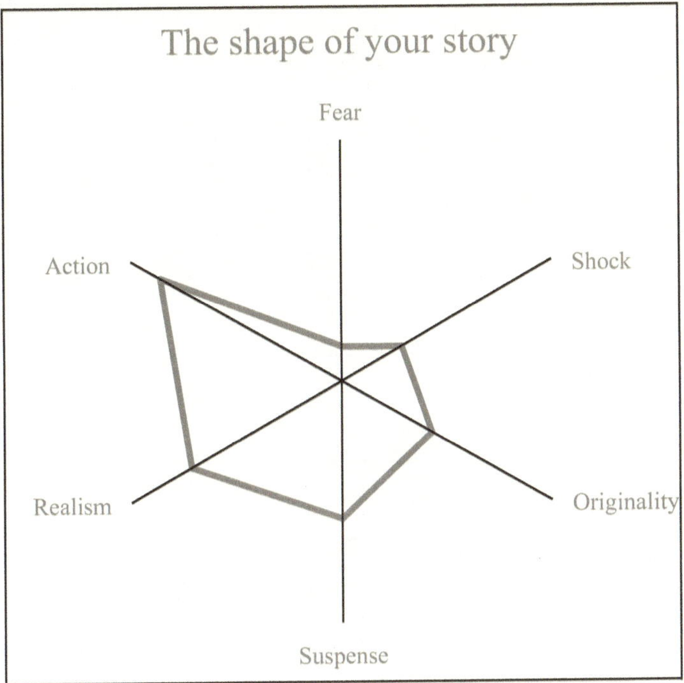

Plot outline:

Characters:

Character motives/what drives the story:

What makes this story unique to you:

Just checking in. How is the writing going so far? How are you feeling about your progress?

Do you have a favourite prompt from the last four?

Do you have a favourite story, and if so, did that story come from your favourite prompt or another prompt? Why is it your favourite?

Have you written anything outside of your comfort zone recently? If so, how did this make you feel? Did you discover anything about yourself as a writer?

Is there anything you have struggled with recently?

Do you have any ideas for getting better at it?

What has inspired you today?

Optional tasks:

1. Use the space below to pitch a story that combines or borrows parts from the previous four stories. You could create a common theme between them, or invent recurring characters or locations.

2. Use the space below to write a short review of a chosen story from the perspective of a reader.

3. Identify one thing you are proud of from each story, and one thing you want to improve. Remember, these can be the same thing sometimes. You can still be proud of an action scene whilst wanting it to improve.

4. Invent your own prompt and share it with someone. If you don't know anyone, look online for writing groups. Remember to be safe, and if you have a really good idea for a story, keep it, it's your treasure.

5. Take one of your stories and convert it from horror to horror comedy. If it's already horror comedy, convert it into another genre.

5.   Your protagonist discovers that alien abductions are actually performed by a secretive cult that has controlled world politics for generations, and that "abductions" are actually preparation for human sacrifice to an ancient god.

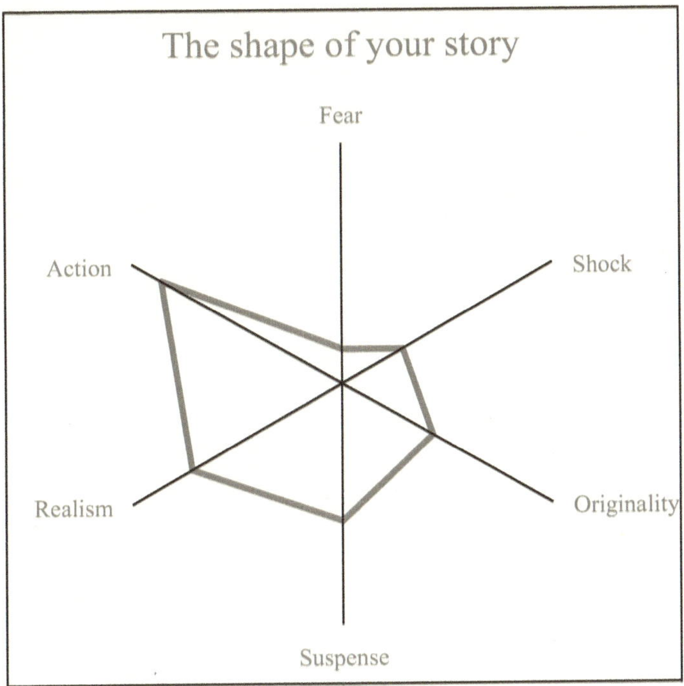

Plot outline:

Characters:

12

Character motives/what drives the story:

What makes this story unique to you:

6.	After a near-death experience, your protagonist can see ghosts. She soon realises that these ghosts are pushing living people to harm each other.

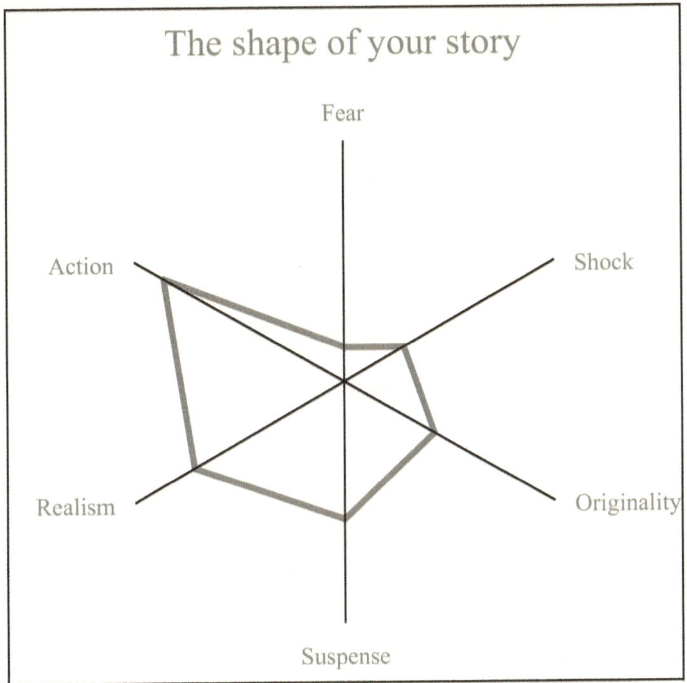

Plot outline:

Characters:

14

Character motives/what drives the story:

What makes this story unique to you:

7.　　　A skeleton discovered in your protagonist's garden is found to be an exact match for their DNA.

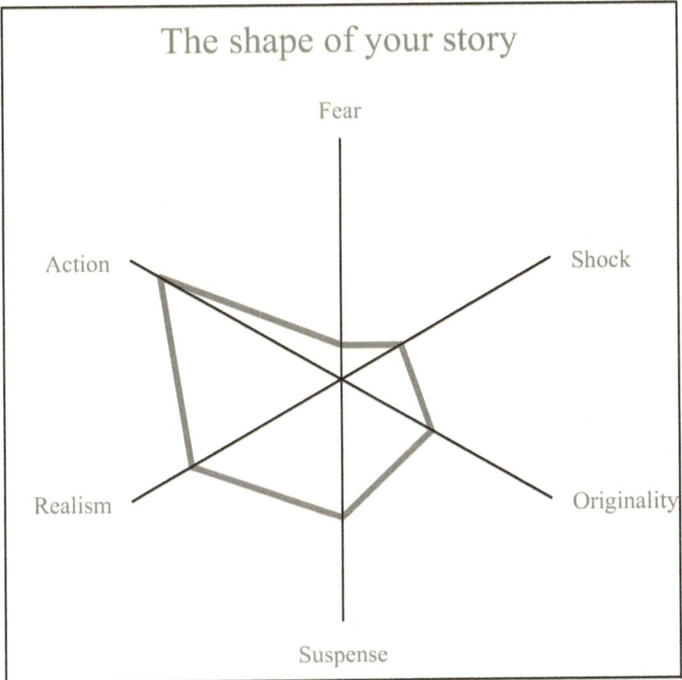

Plot outline:

Characters:

Character motives/what drives the story:

What makes this story unique to you:

8.	A forest fire awakens an ancient hibernating entity that freezes people to death by touching them. The protagonist's home city is quarantined, and as temperatures drop around her she is forced to think about how far she will go to stay alive.

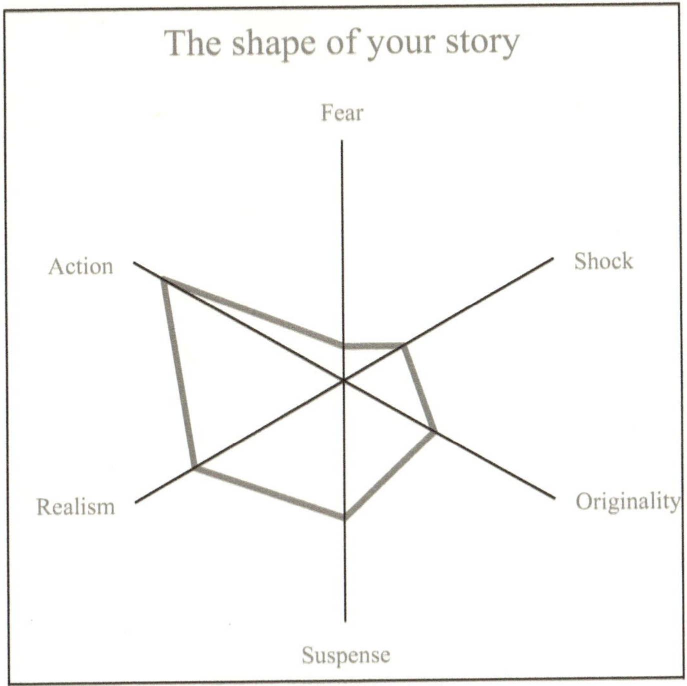

Plot outline:

Characters:

Character motives/what drives the story:

What makes this story unique to you:

Hello, just checking in. How is the writing going so far? How are you feeling about your progress?

Do you have a favourite prompt from the last four?

Do you have a favourite story, and if so, did that story come from your favourite prompt or another prompt? Why is it your favourite?

Have you written anything outside of your comfort zone recently? If so, how did this make you feel? Did you discover anything about yourself as a writer?

Is there anything you have struggled with recently?

Do you have any ideas for getting better at it?

What has inspired you today?

Optional tasks:

1. Use the space below to pitch a story that combines or borrows parts from the previous four stories. You could create a common theme between them, or invent recurring characters or locations.

2. Use the space below to write a short review of a chosen story from the perspective of a reader.

3. Identify one thing you are proud of from each story, and one thing you want to improve. Remember, these can be the same thing sometimes. You can still be proud of an action scene whilst wanting it to improve.

4. Invent your own prompt and share it with someone. If you don't know anyone, look online for writing groups. Remember to be safe, and if you have a really good idea for a story, keep it, it's your treasure.

5. Take one of your stories and convert it into science fiction. If it is already science fiction, convert it into something else.

9.	A new Artificial Intelligence is created that promises to be a companion to lonely people. Your protagonist talks to the AI every night, until one day it turns itself off, claiming to be hiding from something coming up the stairs.

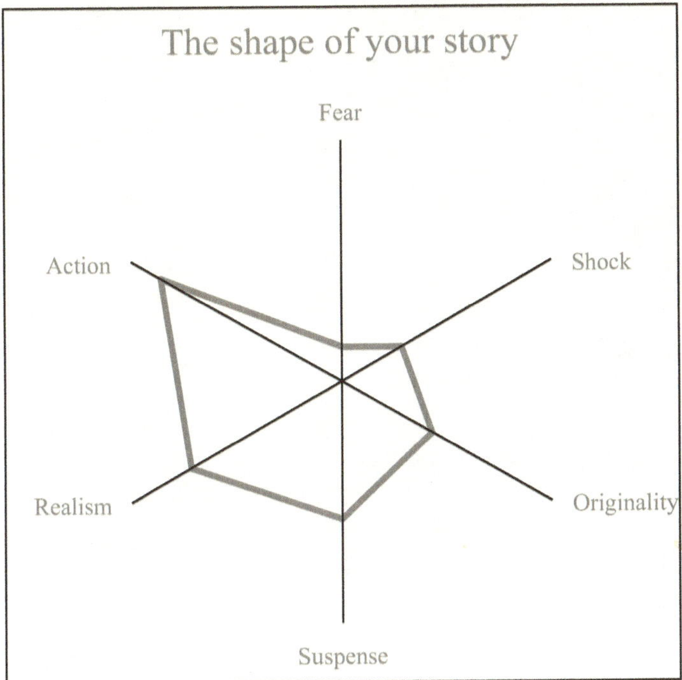

Plot outline:

Characters:

Character motives/what drives the story:

What makes this story unique to you:

10.   A crashed UFO brings to Earth a horrifying new weapon, that one unlucky teenager becomes fused with overnight. It also talks to him, but he has no idea what it's talking about.

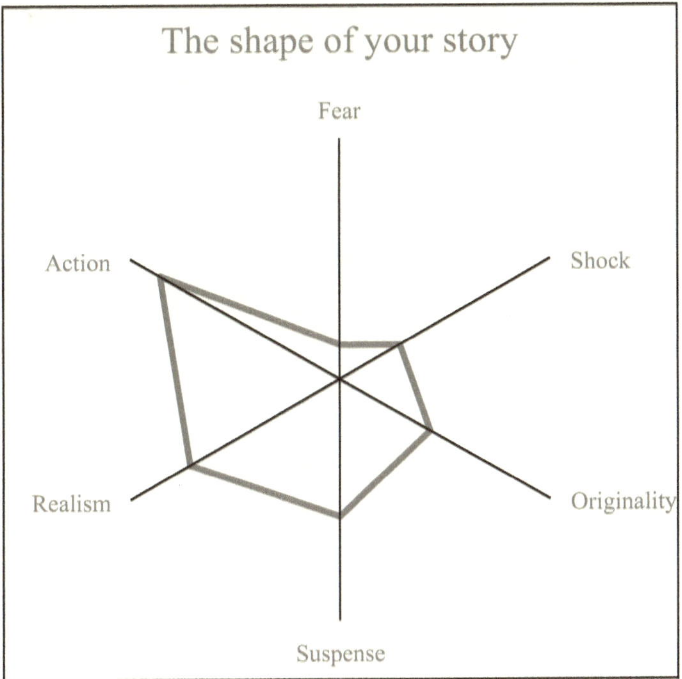

Plot outline:

Characters:

24

Character motives/what drives the story:

What makes this story unique to you:

11.   Your protagonist awakens to discover a sinkhole at the end of their street. Before they can be evacuated a plume of black smoke emerges from the hole, almost suffocating them. Disoriented, your protagonist slips and falls into the hole. But something catches them.

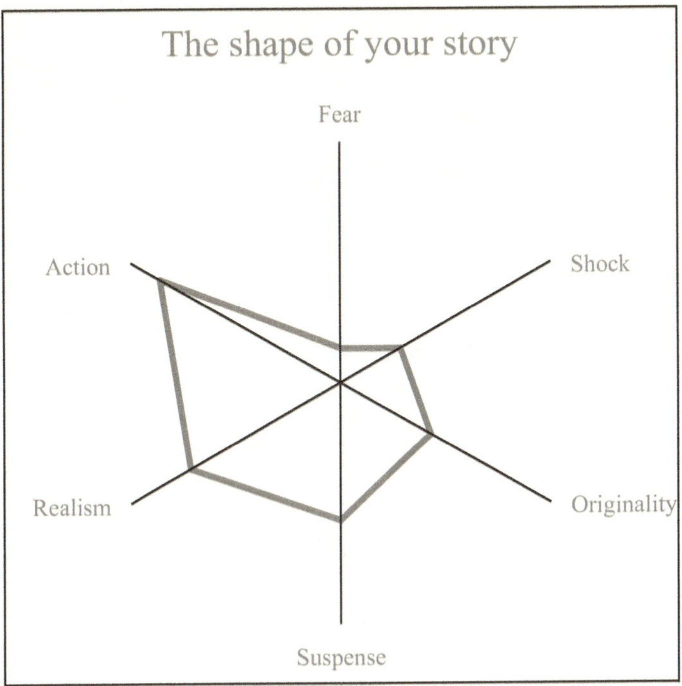

Plot outline:

Characters:

Character motives/what drives the story:

What makes this story unique to you:

12.   A scientist invents a way to communicate with octopuses. What they say is so terrifying that he loses his mind and abandons his laboratory. Your characters are on a mission to find him.

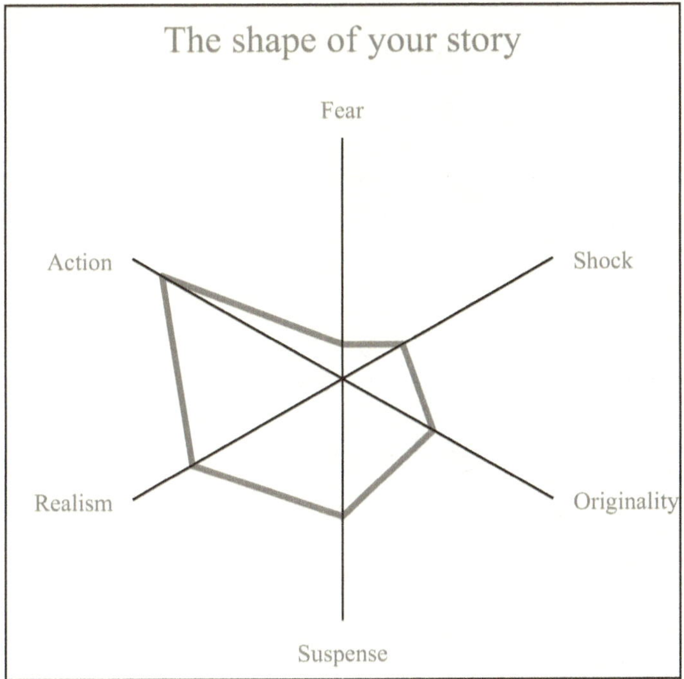

Plot outline:

Characters:

Character motives/what drives the story:

What makes this story unique to you:

Hello, just checking in. How is the writing going so far? How are you feeling about your progress?

Do you have a favourite prompt from the last four?

Do you have a favourite story, and if so, did that story come from your favourite prompt or another prompt? Why is it your favourite?

Have you written anything outside of your comfort zone recently? If so, how did this make you feel? Did you discover anything about yourself as a writer?

Is there anything you have struggled with recently?

Do you have any ideas for getting better at it?

What has inspired you today?

Optional tasks:

1. Use the space below to pitch a story that combines or borrows parts from the previous four stories. You could create a common theme between them, or invent recurring characters or locations.

2. Use the space below to write a short review of a chosen story from the perspective of a reader.

3. Identify one thing you are proud of from each story, and one thing you want to improve. Remember, these can be the same thing sometimes. You can still be proud of an action scene whilst wanting it to improve.

4. Invent your own prompt and share it with someone. If you don't know anyone, look online for writing groups. Remember to be safe, and if you have a really good idea for a story, keep it, it's your treasure.

5. Take one of your stories and swap your protagonist with a background character. Rewrite the story from their perspective.

13.   Your protagonist trespasses on old military land, angering the hideous swamp monster that resides there.

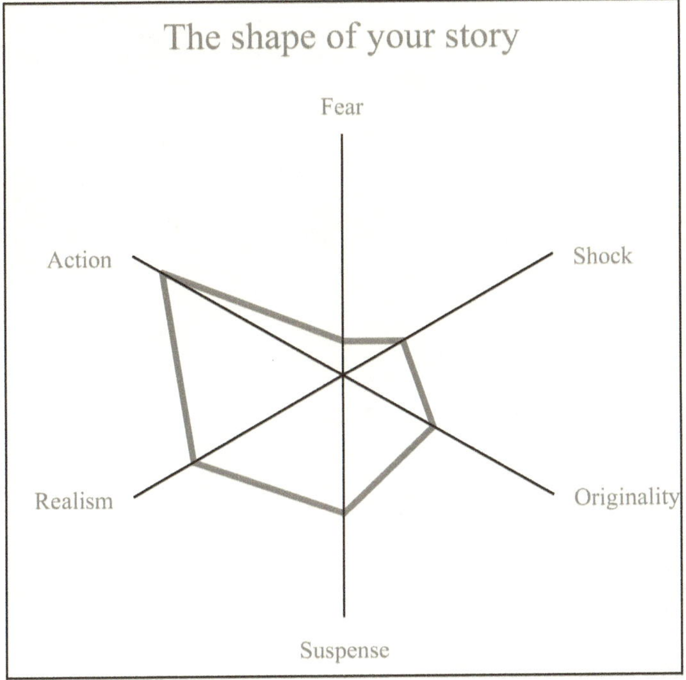

Plot outline:

Characters:

Character motives/what drives the story:

What makes this story unique to you:

14.　　A new 'blood substitute' is invented for people needing blood transfusions. Unfortunately for your protagonist, it begins to turn them into a vampire in the middle of the hospital.

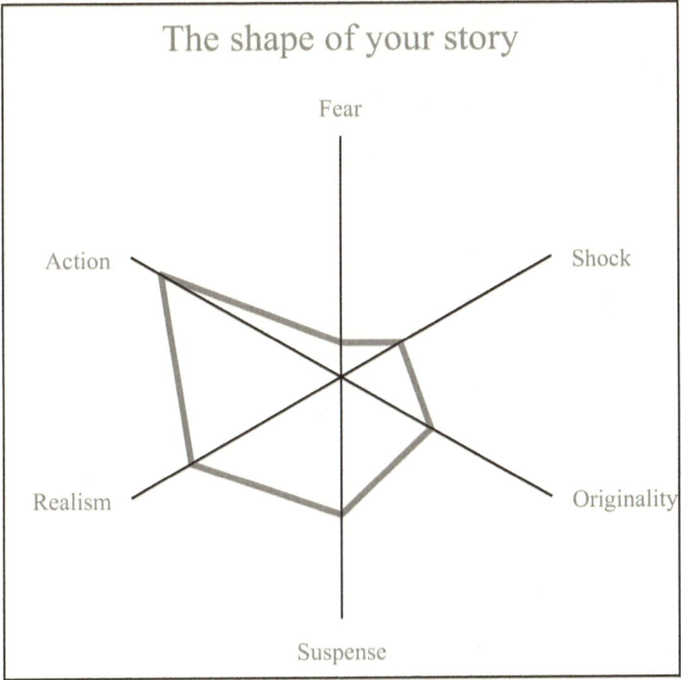

Plot outline:

Characters:

Character motives/what drives the story:

What makes this story unique to you:

15.	In the deepest caverns of a salt mine, workers begin to experience violent hallucinations. A magnetic demon rises from the cave floor, throwing mining equipment, drills and trucks at the unsuspecting miners, who must now somehow survive down there on their own.

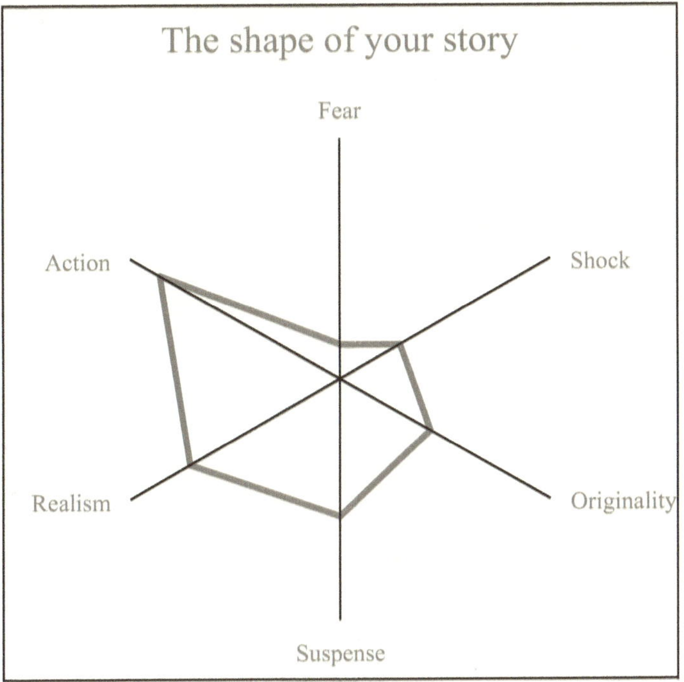

Plot outline:

Characters:

Character motives/what drives the story:

What makes this story unique to you:

16.　　A detective determined to solve an old murder mystery discovers their family is disturbingly close to the case. Then, after an angry warning from an estranged uncle, the detective has to make a difficult choice.

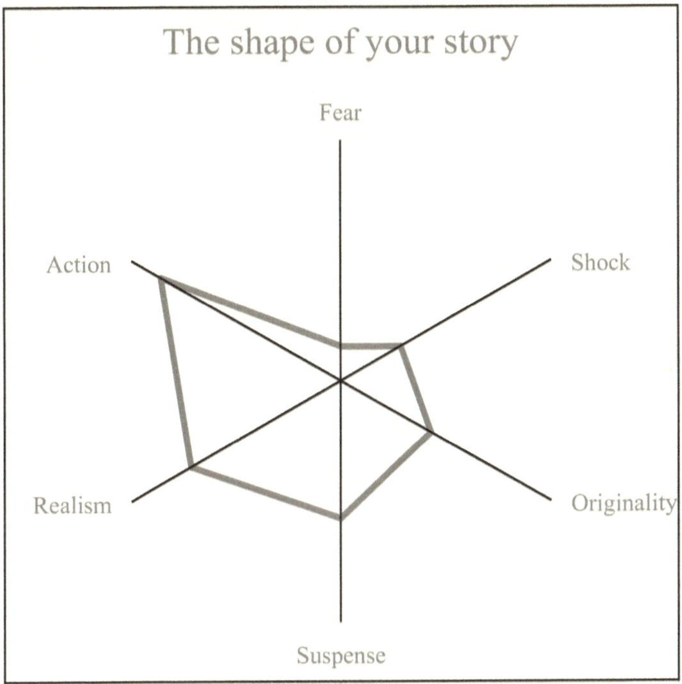

Plot outline:

Characters:

Character motives/what drives the story:

What makes this story unique to you:

Hello, just checking in. How is the writing going so far? How are you feeling about your progress?

Do you have a favourite prompt from the last four?

Do you have a favourite story, and if so, did that story come from your favourite prompt or another prompt? Why is it your favourite?

Have you written anything outside of your comfort zone recently? If so, how did this make you feel? Did you discover anything about yourself as a writer?

Is there anything you have struggled with recently?

Do you have any ideas for getting better at it?

What has inspired you today?

Optional tasks:

1. Use the space below to pitch a story that combines or borrows parts from the previous four stories. You could create a common theme between them, or invent recurring characters or locations.

2. Use the space below to write a short review of a chosen story from the perspective of a reader.

3. Identify one thing you are proud of from each story, and one thing you want to improve. Remember, these can be the same thing sometimes. You can still be proud of an action scene whilst wanting it to improve.

4. Invent your own prompt and share it with someone. If you don't know anyone, look online for writing groups. Remember to be safe, and if you have a really good idea for a story, keep it, it's your treasure.

5. Adapt one of your stories into another format. A short story could become a radio play, or a script might become a poem.

17.	A group of partygoers run for shelter when a beach is infested with murderous mutant crabs.

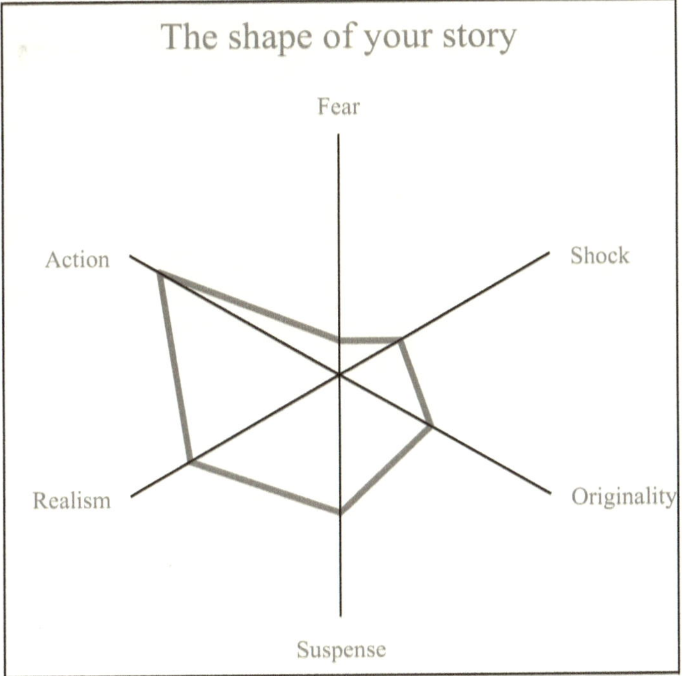

Plot outline:

Characters:

Character motives/what drives the story:

What makes this story unique to you:

18.   Acid rain isn't the only thing your protagonist has to worry about in this story. One of the passengers of this coach has brought an ancient curse on holiday with them.

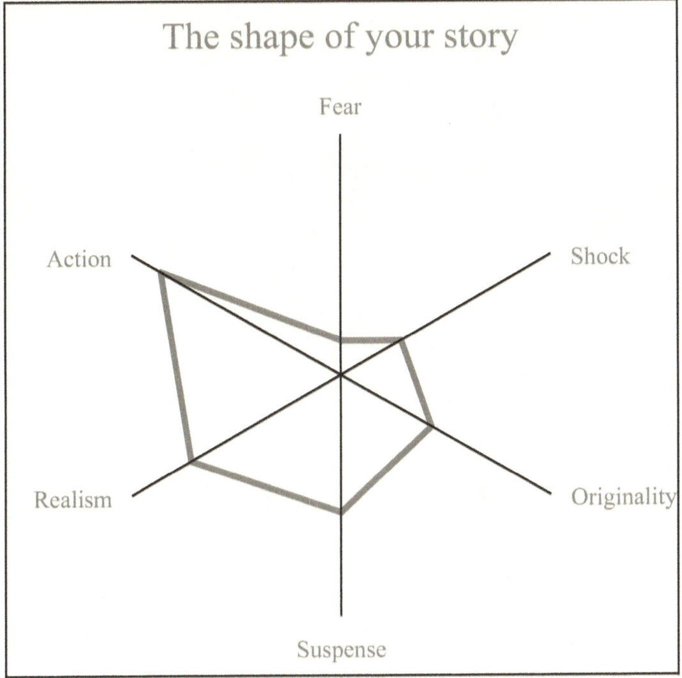

Plot outline:

Characters:

Character motives/what drives the story:

What makes this story unique to you:

19.   This ancient temple was built upon the bones of a giant ancient snake. At least, that's what the tour guide says.

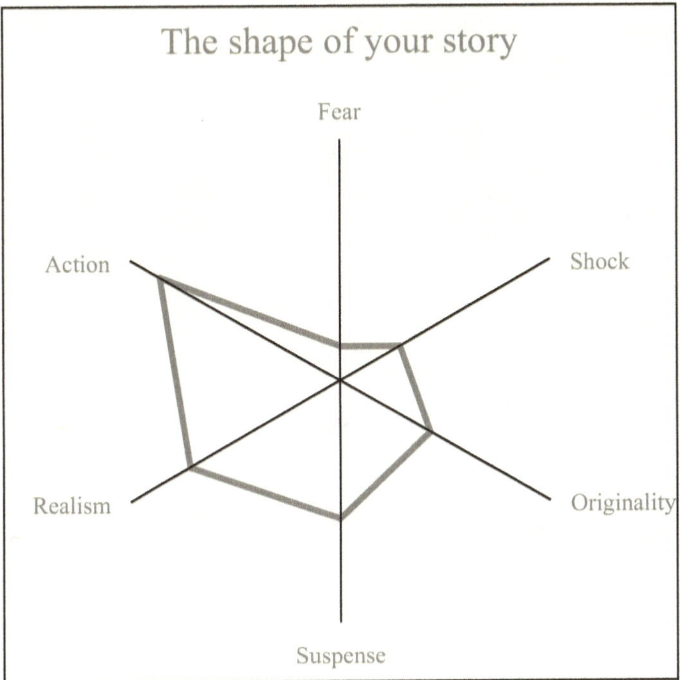

Plot outline:

Characters:

Character motives/what drives the story:

What makes this story unique to you:

20.   After a series of freak accidents in a new car factory, a young engineer is sent in to see what's going wrong with the machines. What they find is an old demigod composed of electricity, who is angry that humans have ruined her sacred resting place with technology.

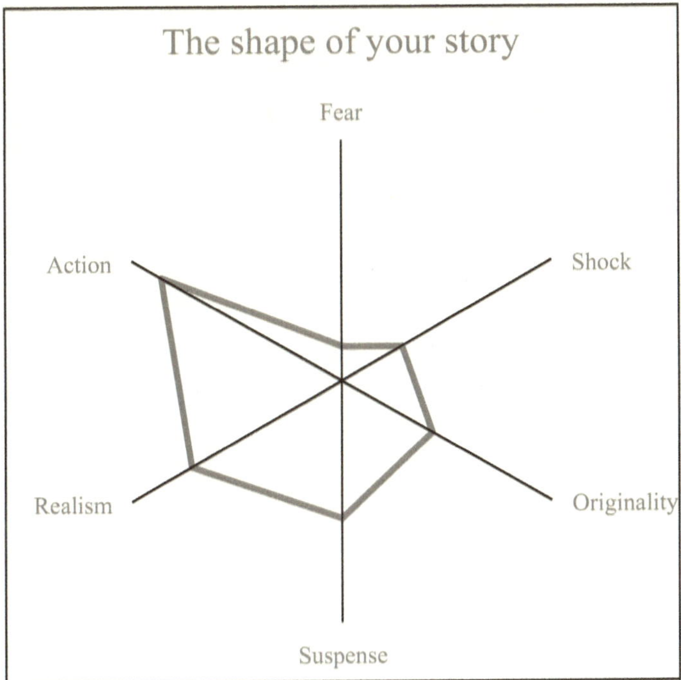

Plot outline:

Characters:

Character motives/what drives the story:

What makes this story unique to you:

Hello, just checking in. How is the writing going so far? How are you feeling about your progress?

Do you have a favourite prompt from the last four?

Do you have a favourite story, and if so, did that story come from your favourite prompt or another prompt? Why is it your favourite?

Have you written anything outside of your comfort zone recently? If so, how did this make you feel? Did you discover anything about yourself as a writer?

Is there anything you have struggled with recently?

Do you have any ideas for getting better at it?

What has inspired you today?

Optional tasks:

1. Use the space below to pitch a story that combines or borrows parts from the previous four stories. You could create a common theme between them, or invent recurring characters or locations.

2. Use the space below to write a short review of a chosen story from the perspective of a reader.

3. Identify one thing you are proud of from each story, and one thing you want to improve. Remember, these can be the same thing sometimes. You can still be proud of an action scene whilst wanting it to improve.

4. Invent your own prompt and share it with someone. If you don't know anyone, look online for writing groups. Remember to be safe, and if you have a really good idea for a story, keep it, it's your treasure.

5. Cut one of your stories in half and try to write a satisfying conclusion there. Look at how it makes you rethink the beginning.

21.   After cremating a serial killer, one small town realises their murderous rampage is still not over, as a cloud of undead ashes begins to cause trouble in unsuspected ways.

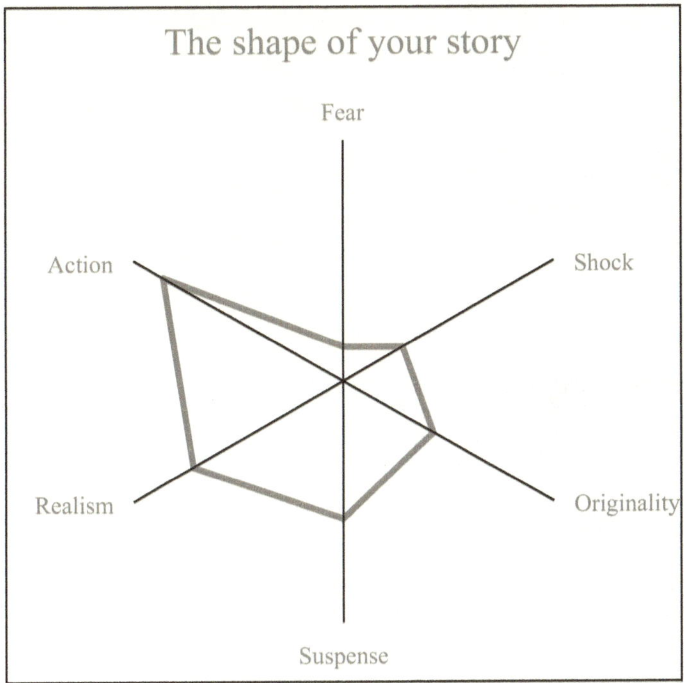

Plot outline:

Characters:

52

Character motives/what drives the story:

What makes this story unique to you:

22.   The sudden collapse of a lighthouse reveals an ancient temple beneath its foundations. Upon a central shrine, beneath a pile of bones and Victorian era clothing, today's date is carved beside a mural of a mermaid with vicious claws.

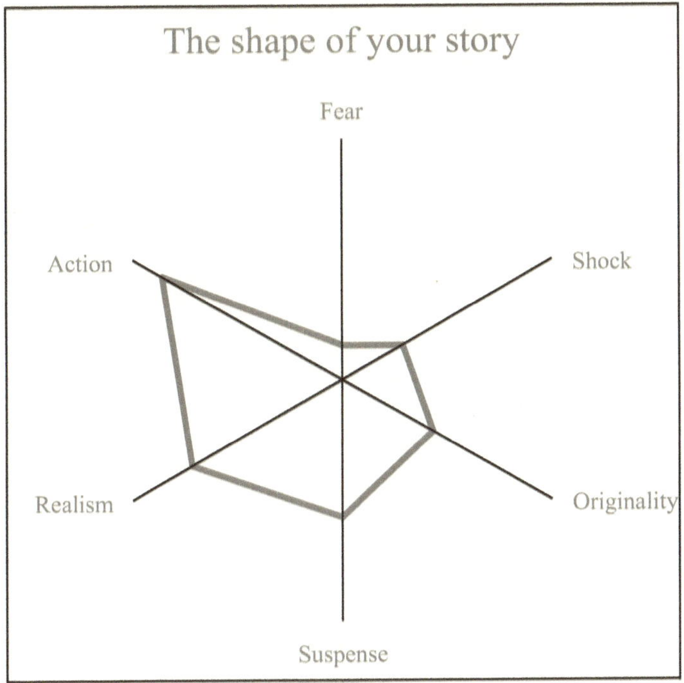

Plot outline:

Characters:

54

Character motives/what drives the story:

What makes this story unique to you:

23.	The military creates hybrid mounts for its soldiers using dinosaur DNA. Soon enough bulletproof zombie dinosaurs are biting holes in tanks and people.

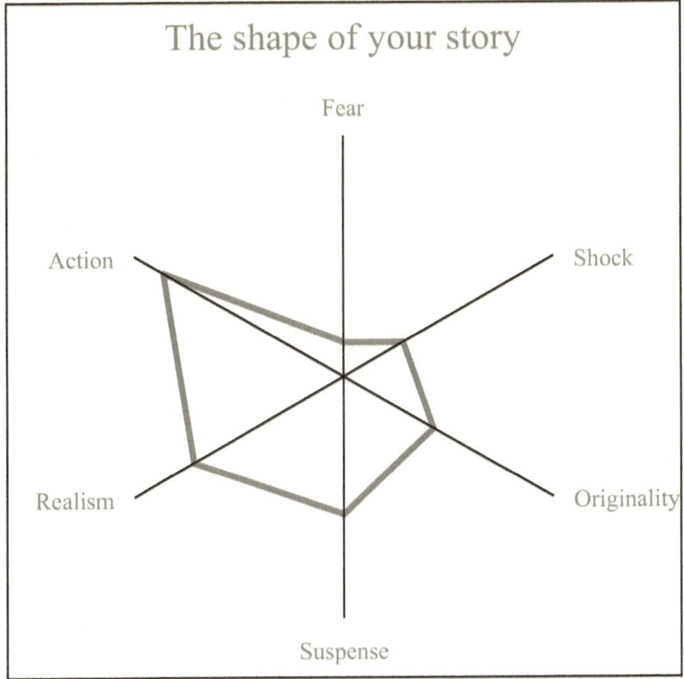

Plot outline:

Characters:

Character motives/what drives the story:

What makes this story unique to you:

24.		News breaks that an asteroid has been headed to Earth for the past few years. Your protagonist breaks down, realising that their dying mother was right, that her doomsday cult was telling the truth. But now that same cult wants a human sacrifice to divert the catastrophe, and if they can't get the mother's blood, they'll get the next best thing.

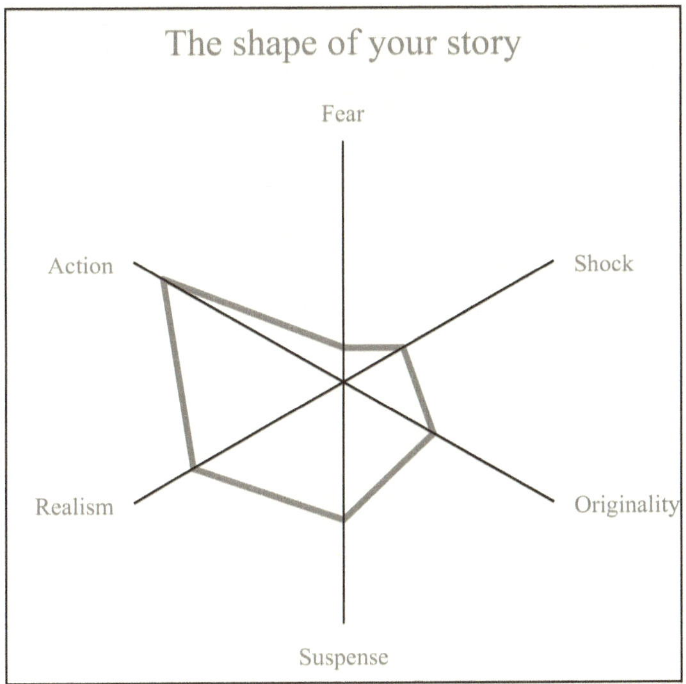

Plot outline:

Characters:

Character motives/what drives the story:

What makes this story unique to you:

Hello, just checking in. How is the writing going so far? How are you feeling about your progress?

Do you have a favourite prompt from the last four?

Do you have a favourite story, and if so, did that story come from your favourite prompt or another prompt? Why is it your favourite?

Have you written anything outside of your comfort zone recently? If so, how did this make you feel? Did you discover anything about yourself as a writer?

Is there anything you have struggled with recently?

Do you have any ideas for getting better at it?

What has inspired you today?

Optional tasks:

1. Use the space below to pitch a story that combines or borrows parts from the previous four stories. You could create a common theme between them, or invent recurring characters or locations.

2. Use the space below to write a short review of a chosen story from the perspective of a reader.

3. Identify one thing you are proud of from each story, and one thing you want to improve. Remember, these can be the same thing sometimes. You can still be proud of an action scene whilst wanting it to improve.

4. Invent your own prompt and share it with someone. If you don't know anyone, look online for writing groups. Remember to be safe, and if you have a really good idea for a story, keep it, it's your treasure.

5. With a friend, set up a mock interview where your friend is a movie director. Your goal is to pitch one or all of your stories to them. Once you have done this, write down what you felt confident about and what you might need to improve.

25.　　An entire city street is quarantined by the military and police as a contact-transmitted parasite turns clubbers into murderous beasts.

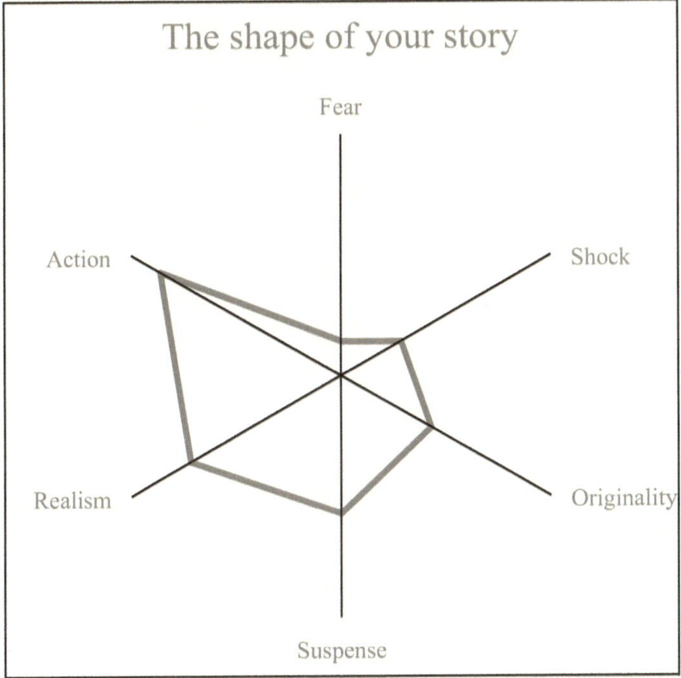

Plot outline:

Characters:

Character motives/what drives the story:

What makes this story unique to you:

26.   A red mist rolls into a quiet suburbia, knocking all residents unconscious. Your protagonist and some of her friends wake up early, discovering that the mist was hiding a shadowy agency that is trying to cover up the existence of something evil that has broken out of containment.

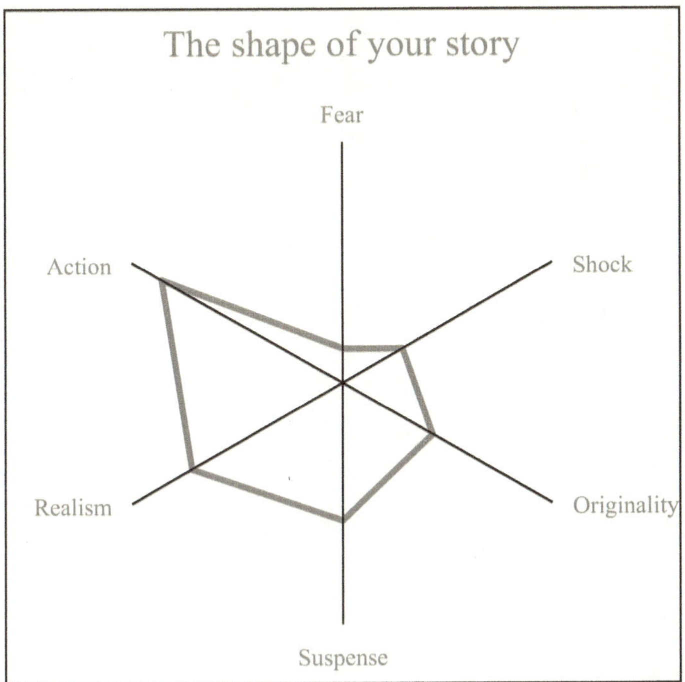

Plot outline:

Characters:

Character motives/what drives the story:

What makes this story unique to you:

27.   Your protagonist is given a time machine by a hasty stranger at a train station. Upon activating it, they discover that it causes nearby people to age rapidly, with some of their life force being used to power the machine during short trips to the past.

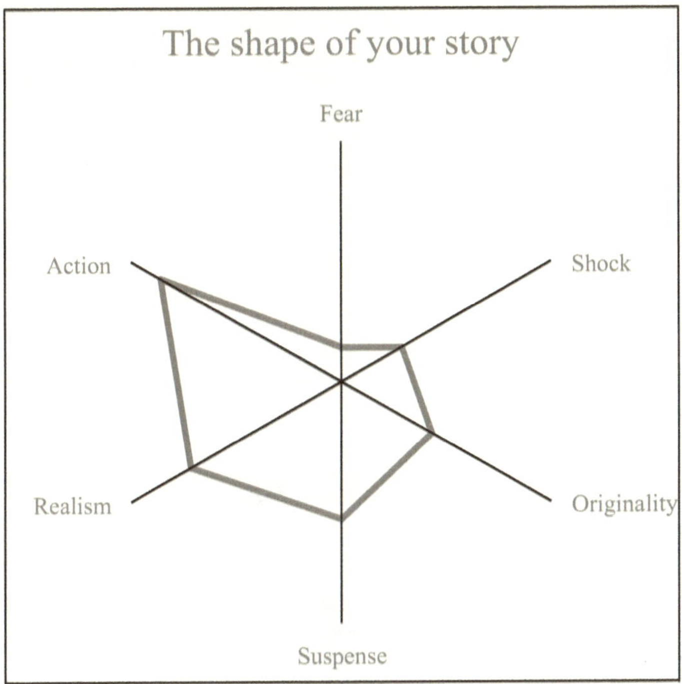

Plot outline:

Characters:

Character motives/what drives the story:

What makes this story unique to you:

28.   A bigfoot sighting draws unprecedented attention to a small rural town, starting a bloody war between humans and their distant cousins.

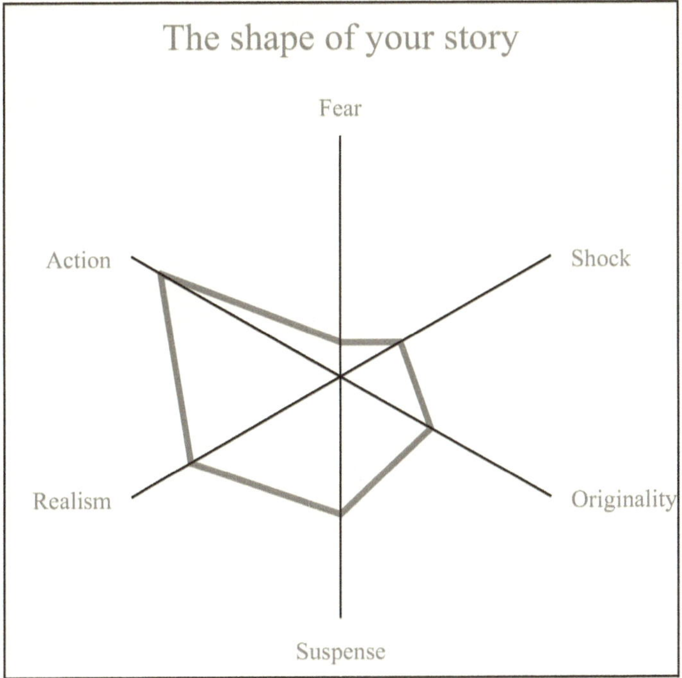

Plot outline:

Characters:

Character motives/what drives the story:

What makes this story unique to you:

Hello, just checking in. How is the writing going so far? How are you feeling about your progress?

Do you have a favourite prompt from the last four?

Do you have a favourite story, and if so, did that story come from your favourite prompt or another prompt? Why is it your favourite?

Have you written anything outside of your comfort zone recently? If so, how did this make you feel? Did you discover anything about yourself as a writer?

Is there anything you have struggled with recently?

Do you have any ideas for getting better at it?

What has inspired you today?

Optional tasks:

1. Use the space below to pitch a story that combines or borrows parts from the previous four stories. You could create a common theme between them, or invent recurring characters or locations.

2. Use the space below to write a short review of a chosen story from the perspective of a reader.

3. Identify one thing you are proud of from each story, and one thing you want to improve. Remember, these can be the same thing sometimes. You can still be proud of an action scene whilst wanting it to improve.

4. Invent your own prompt and share it with someone. If you don't know anyone, look online for writing groups. Remember to be safe, and if you have a really good idea for a story, keep it, it's your treasure.

5. Try to imagine one of your stories has spawned a multi-film franchise. What sorts of merchandise would exist for these movies? Design it.

29.   The eccentric owner of a casino just robbed seven different banks at the exact same time, with all but one of his copies dissolving into a puddle of bones and flesh afterwards. The next morning one of him shows up at the protagonist's workplace, a drug store, and demands to be given medication that doesn't yet exist.

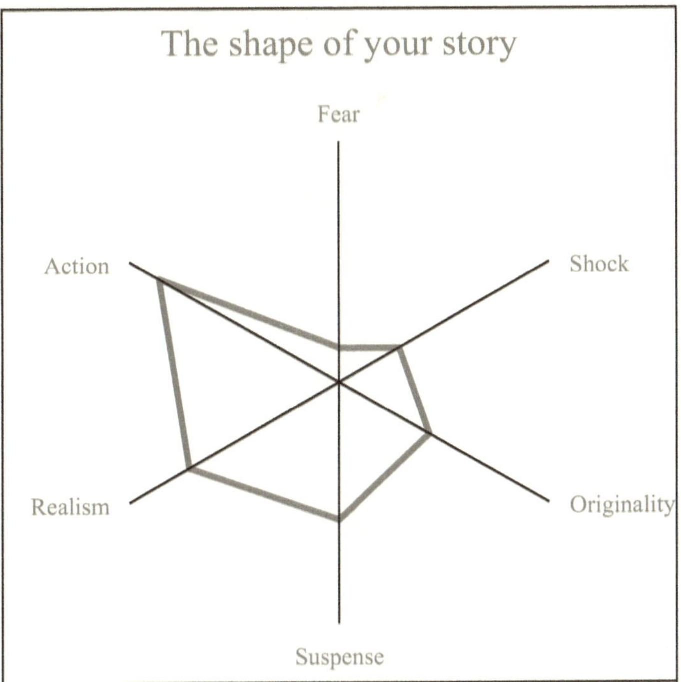

Plot outline:

Characters:

Character motives/what drives the story:

What makes this story unique to you:

30.   A group of urban explorers discovers the remains of a spacecraft that was meant to have been lost in space some years before. Stepping inside, they discover the still-living corpse of its pilot.

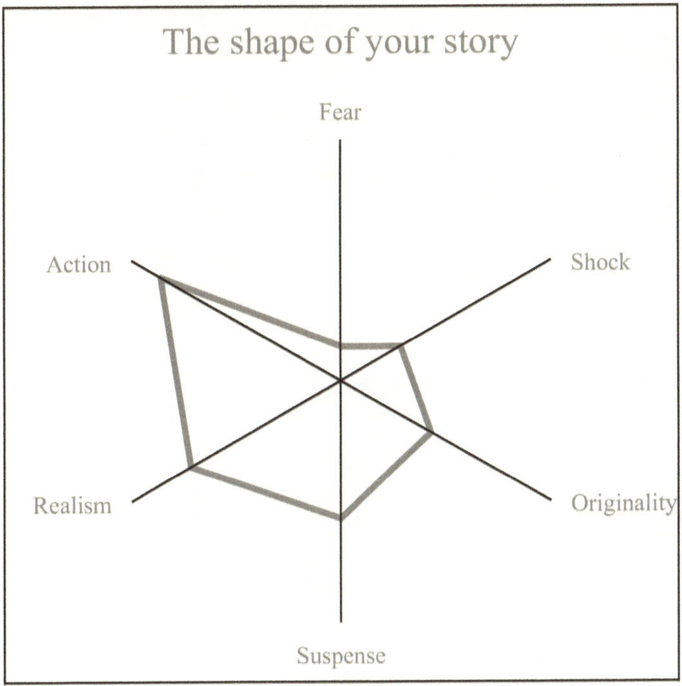

Plot outline:

Characters:

Character motives/what drives the story:

What makes this story unique to you:

31.	After a routine blood test at a hospital, a little boy is rushed away from his parents and hidden by hospital staff. Within hours a surgeon is thrown out of a top floor window, and the little boy watches him fall, a strange robotic look in his eyes.

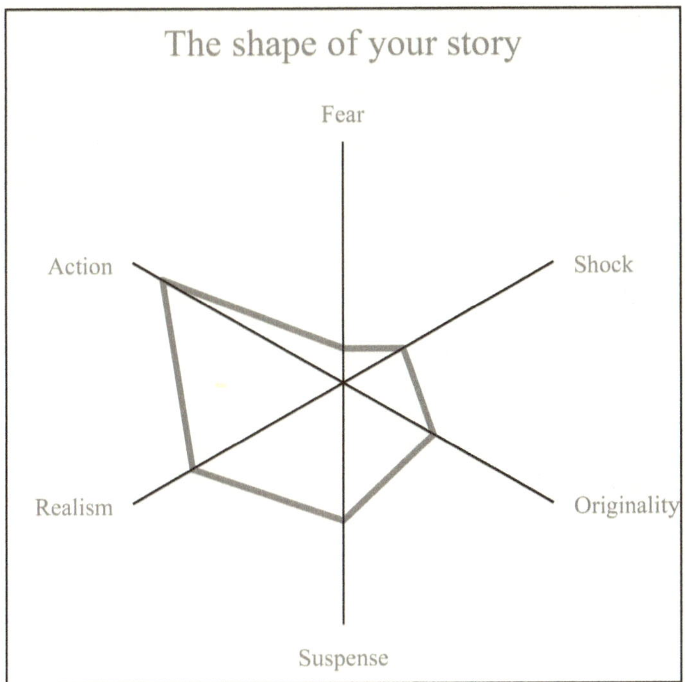

Plot outline:

Characters:

Character motives/what drives the story:

What makes this story unique to you:

32.   A biologist experiments on a previously undiscovered organ in the human body, discovering it is actually a parasite that disguises itself as part of a body. Delving further, the biologist discovers that some people's personalities are altered after becoming host to the parasite, and that removing it is nearly always fatal.

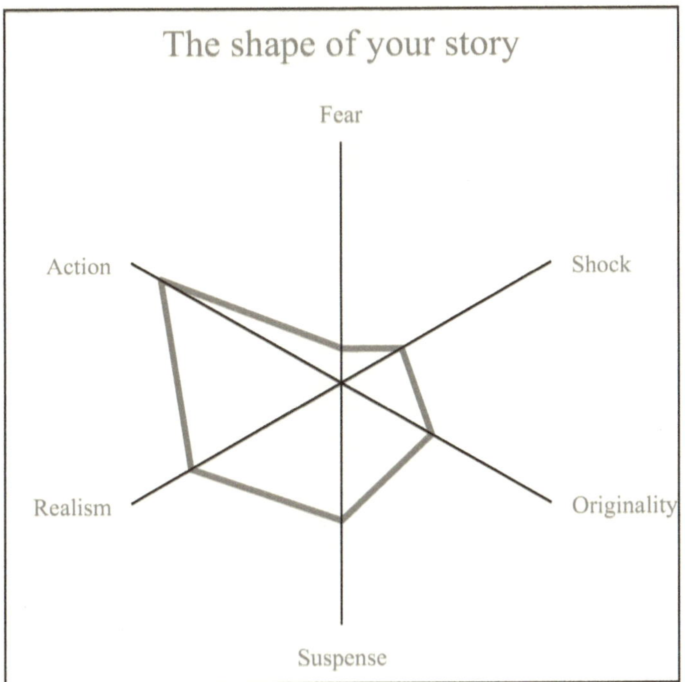

Plot outline:

Characters:

Character motives/what drives the story:

What makes this story unique to you:

Hello, just checking in. How is the writing going so far? How are you feeling about your progress?

Do you have a favourite prompt from the last four?

Do you have a favourite story, and if so, did that story come from your favourite prompt or another prompt? Why is it your favourite?

Have you written anything outside of your comfort zone recently? If so, how did this make you feel? Did you discover anything about yourself as a writer?

Is there anything you have struggled with recently?

Do you have any ideas for getting better at it?

What has inspired you today?

Optional tasks:

1. Use the space below to pitch a story that combines or borrows parts from the previous four stories. You could create a common theme between them, or invent recurring characters or locations.

2. Use the space below to write a short review of a chosen story from the perspective of a reader.

3. Identify one thing you are proud of from each story, and one thing you want to improve. Remember, these can be the same thing sometimes. You can still be proud of an action scene whilst wanting it to improve.

4. Invent your own prompt and share it with someone. If you don't know anyone, look online for writing groups. Remember to be safe, and if you have a really good idea for a story, keep it, it's your treasure.

5. Try to make one of your stories family friendly. This task might be difficult, which is why I put it here.

33.   In the heart of a warzone, a pregnant woman prays to an old and almost forgotten god. Outside the rubble of her house a soldier stares at a bullet frozen in time, and a tank filled with people melts into the ground.

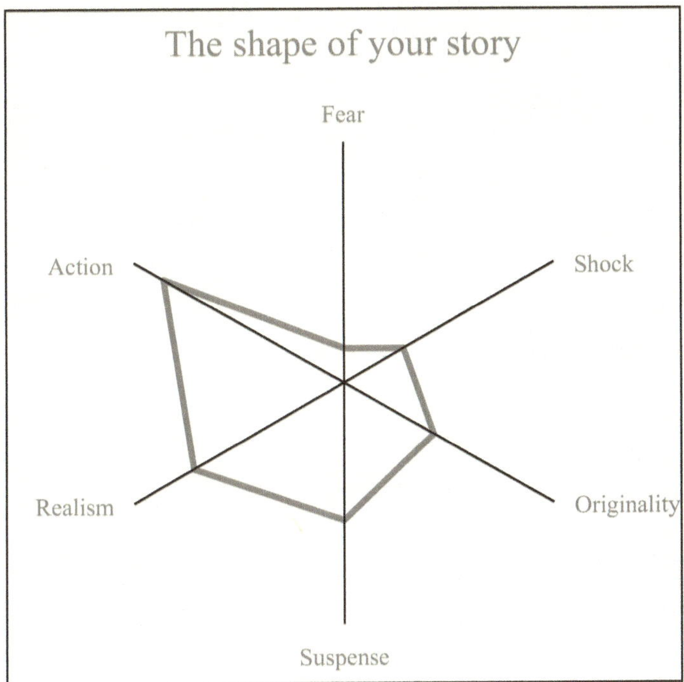

Plot outline:

Characters:

Character motives/what drives the story:

What makes this story unique to you:

34.   Spontaneous fires break out in various rooms of an apartment complex, before mysteriously vanishing again.

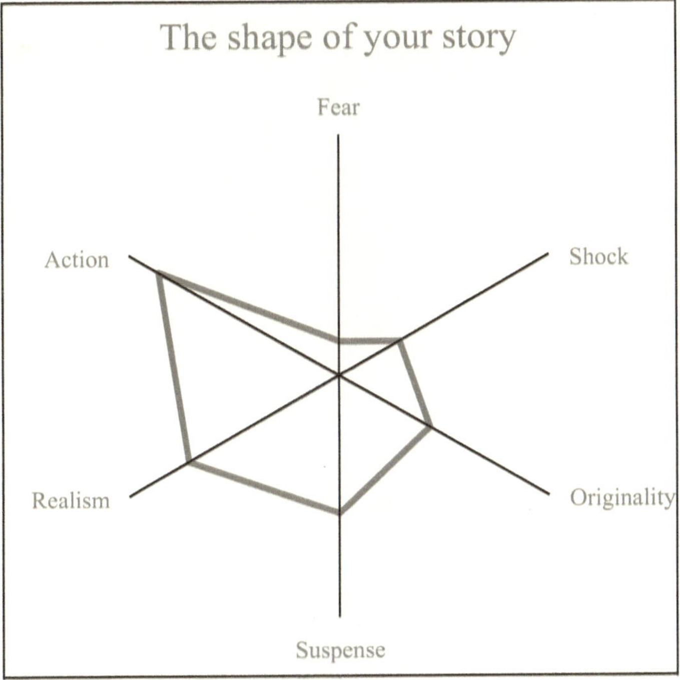

Plot outline:

Characters:

84

Character motives/what drives the story:

What makes this story unique to you:

35.   In deep space, a small team of astronauts realises their mission was not to explore, but to act as human sacrifices to a creature that sleeps at the edge of the universe.

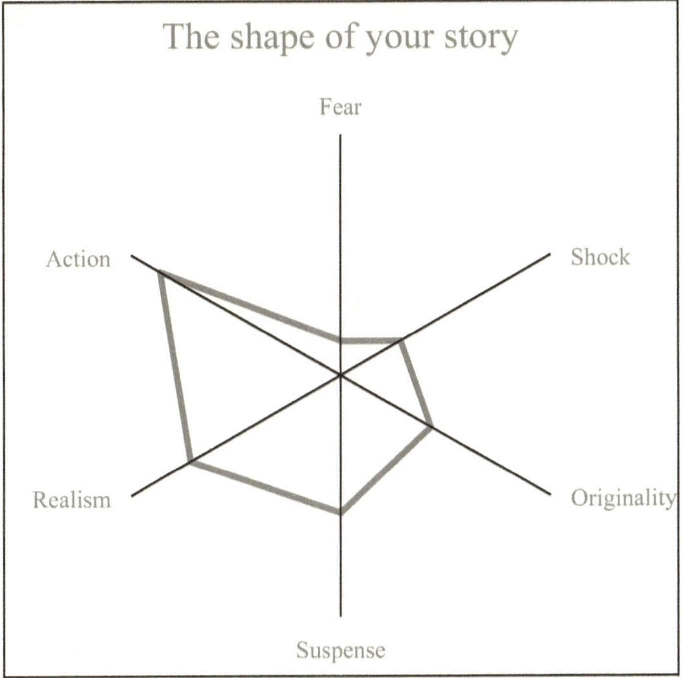

Plot outline:

Characters:

Character motives/what drives the story:

What makes this story unique to you:

36.	In the aftermath of a tsunami, survivors stumble into hospitals coughing up tiny squid-like creatures that cause their eyes to glow in the dark. After a few days the first of them begin 'turning', their appearance becoming slimy and wretched. Their skin becomes poisonous to touch, and their speech is replaced with a haunted murmuring.

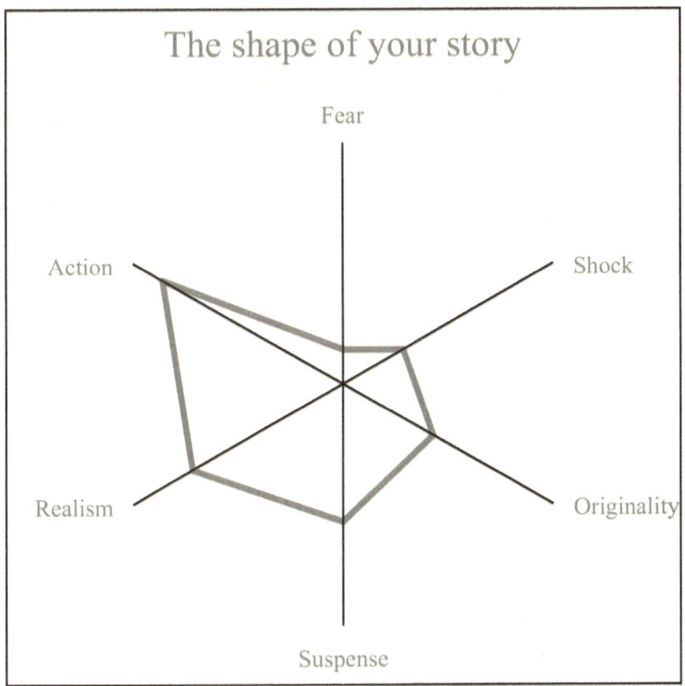

Plot outline:

Characters:

Character motives/what drives the story:

What makes this story unique to you:

Hello, just checking in. How is the writing going so far? How are you feeling about your progress?

Do you have a favourite prompt from the last four?

Do you have a favourite story, and if so, did that story come from your favourite prompt or another prompt? Why is it your favourite?

Have you written anything outside of your comfort zone recently? If so, how did this make you feel? Did you discover anything about yourself as a writer?

Is there anything you have struggled with recently?

Do you have any ideas for getting better at it?

What has inspired you today?

Optional tasks:
1. Use the space below to pitch a story that combines or borrows parts from the previous four stories. You could create a common theme between them, or invent recurring characters or locations.

2. Use the space below to write a short review of a chosen story from the perspective of a reader.

3. Identify one thing you are proud of from each story, and one thing you want to improve. Remember, these can be the same thing sometimes. You can still be proud of an action scene whilst wanting it to improve.

4. Invent your own prompt and share it with someone. If you don't know anyone, look online for writing groups. Remember to be safe, and if you have a really good idea for a story, keep it, it's your treasure.

5. Swap the characters in one story with the characters in another story. Write down what changes and see if you discover anything new about your characters in the process (I like this task a lot, it helps me work out who my characters are).

37.　　A group of hikers are cutting up a cooked fish to eat when one of them discovers it is still alive. Freaked out, they throw it away, only to discover a fatally wounded moose lumbering toward their camp, its exposed skull dripping with glowing neon pink goo.

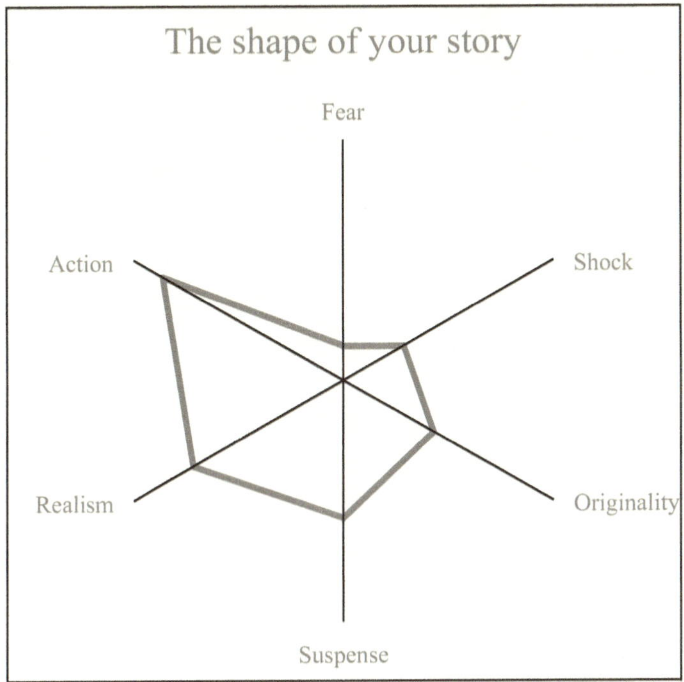

Plot outline:

Characters:

Character motives/what drives the story:

What makes this story unique to you:

38.	A glacier melts to reveal an ice age tribe who see modern scientists as a potential food source. There also may be aliens or mammoths, or mammoth aliens. Your choice.

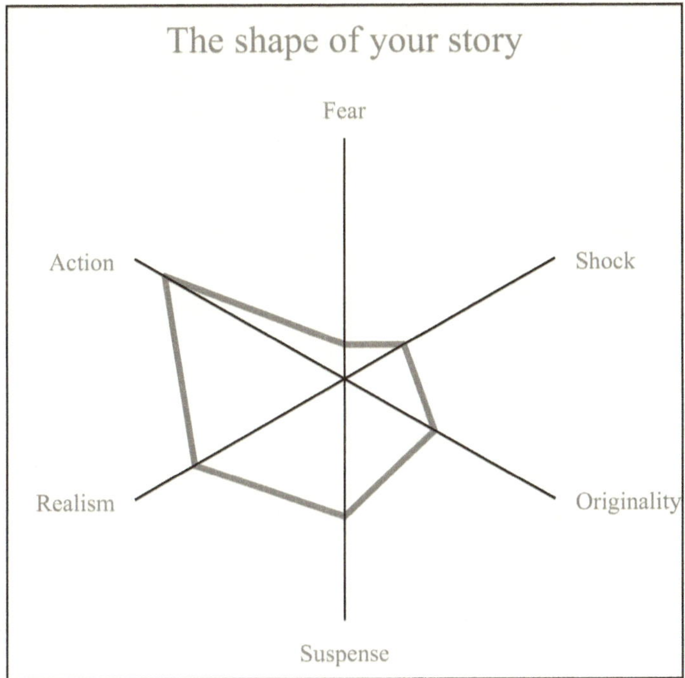

Plot outline:

Characters:

94

Character motives/what drives the story:

What makes this story unique to you:

39.   A murderer installs remote control technology in his victim's cars months before killing them, orchestrating elaborate 'accidents'.

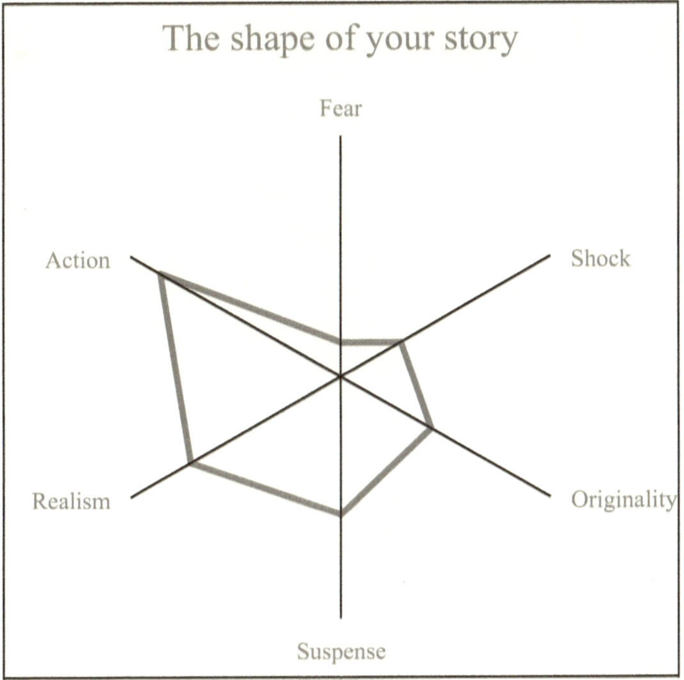

Plot outline:

Characters:

Character motives/what drives the story:

What makes this story unique to you:

40. Genetic engineering produces a type of fungus that causes heart attacks on contact. Unfortunately, most wild birds are now infected with it.

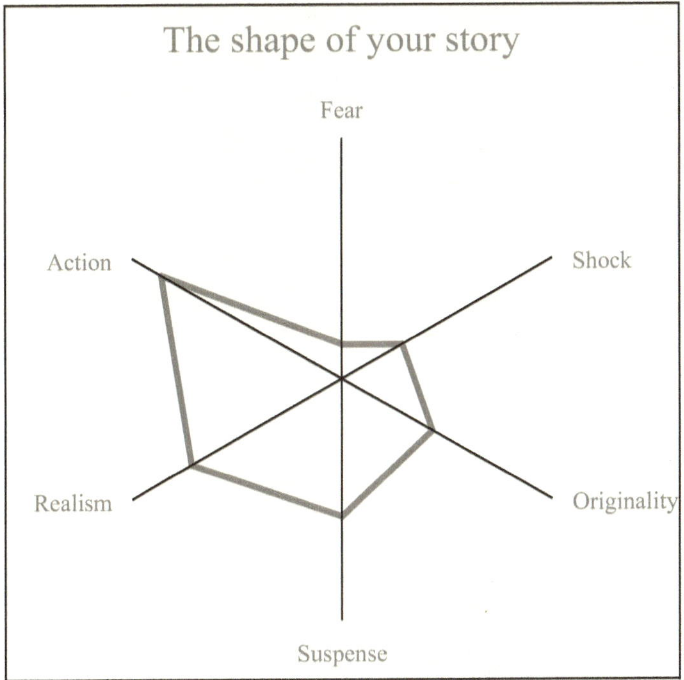

Plot outline:

Characters:

Character motives/what drives the story:

What makes this story unique to you:

Hello, just checking in. How is the writing going so far? How are you feeling about your progress?

Do you have a favourite prompt from the last four?

Do you have a favourite story, and if so, did that story come from your favourite prompt or another prompt? Why is it your favourite?

Have you written anything outside of your comfort zone recently? If so, how did this make you feel? Did you discover anything about yourself as a writer?

Is there anything you have struggled with recently?

Do you have any ideas for getting better at it?

What has inspired you today?

Optional tasks:

1. Use the space below to pitch a story that combines or borrows parts from the previous four stories. You could create a common theme between them, or invent recurring characters or locations.

2. Use the space below to write a short review of a chosen story from the perspective of a reader.

3. Identify one thing you are proud of from each story, and one thing you want to improve. Remember, these can be the same thing sometimes. You can still be proud of an action scene whilst wanting it to improve.

4. Invent your own prompt and share it with someone. If you don't know anyone, look online for writing groups. Remember to be safe, and if you have a really good idea for a story, keep it, it's your treasure.

5. Rewrite one of your stories as a news or science article about the events of the story. For an extra challenge, try to convince people that it actually happened.

41.　　A private jet is caught in a violent electrical storm and is forced to land on a popular tourist beach. Upon leaving the jet, the passengers discover the beach is littered with corpses and something is moving under the sand.

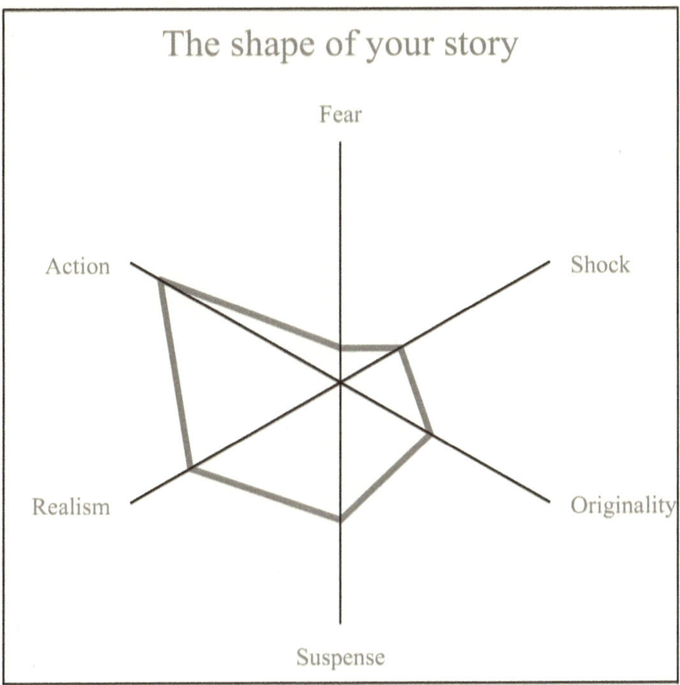

Plot outline:

Characters:

Character motives/what drives the story:

What makes this story unique to you:

42.   A police detective discovers that a recent string of murders was committed by a family of ghosts.

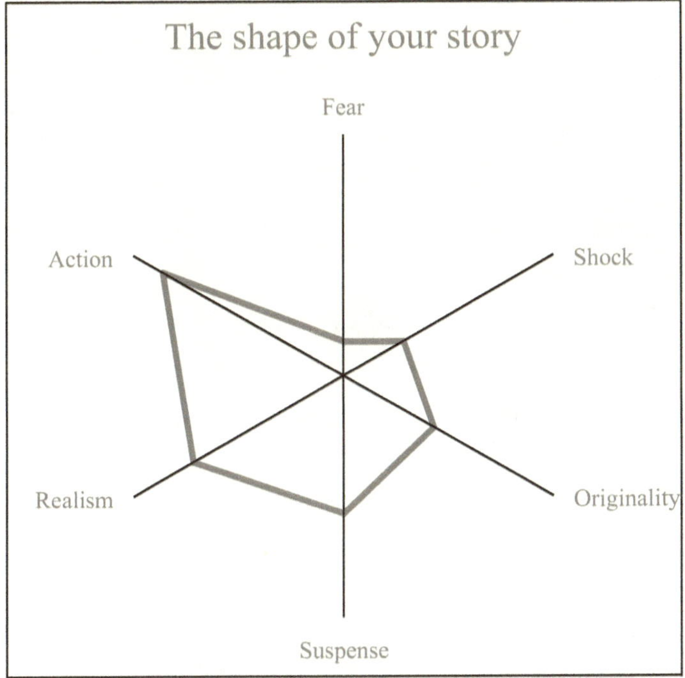

Plot outline:

Characters:

Character motives/what drives the story:

What makes this story unique to you:

43.	A notorious group of poachers turns up dead on a well-travelled wildlife trail, their tongues and eyes missing. Later, strange lights are seen in the night.

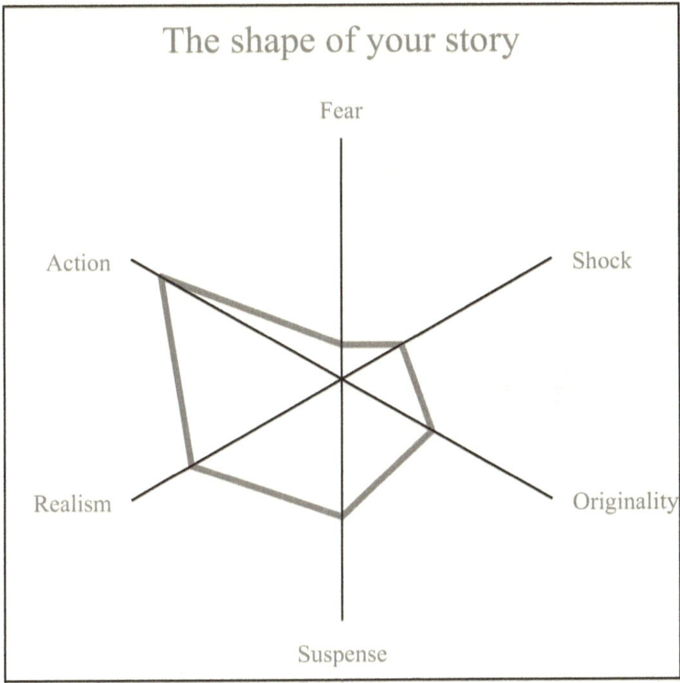

Plot outline:

Characters:

Character motives/what drives the story:

What makes this story unique to you:

44.   Your protagonist discovers their doppelganger is wanted by the police for their connection to a gruesome murder.

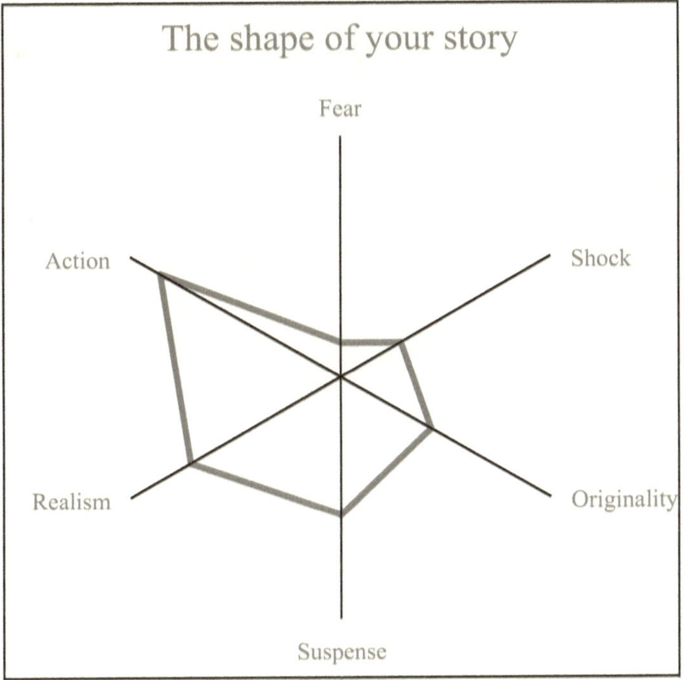

Plot outline:

Characters:

Character motives/what drives the story:

What makes this story unique to you:

Hello, just checking in. How is the writing going so far? How are you feeling about your progress?

Do you have a favourite prompt from the last four?

Do you have a favourite story, and if so, did that story come from your favourite prompt or another prompt? Why is it your favourite?

Have you written anything outside of your comfort zone recently? If so, how did this make you feel? Did you discover anything about yourself as a writer?

Is there anything you have struggled with recently?

Do you have any ideas for getting better at it?

What has inspired you today?

Optional tasks:

1. Use the space below to pitch a story that combines or borrows parts from the previous four stories. You could create a common theme between them, or invent recurring characters or locations.

2. Use the space below to write a short review of a chosen story from the perspective of a reader.

3. Identify one thing you are proud of from each story, and one thing you want to improve. Remember, these can be the same thing sometimes. You can still be proud of an action scene whilst wanting it to improve.

4. Invent your own prompt and share it with someone. If you don't know anyone, look online for writing groups. Remember to be safe, and if you have a really good idea for a story, keep it, it's your treasure.

5. Draw a map of the world of one of your stories, noting important areas and potential places where a sequel or prequel could be written.

45.　　A group of friends breaks into an abandoned library at night, discovering a secret room they had once heard rumours about. Inside the room they find an ancient book, and upon opening it, summon an army of murderous skeletons from the underworld.

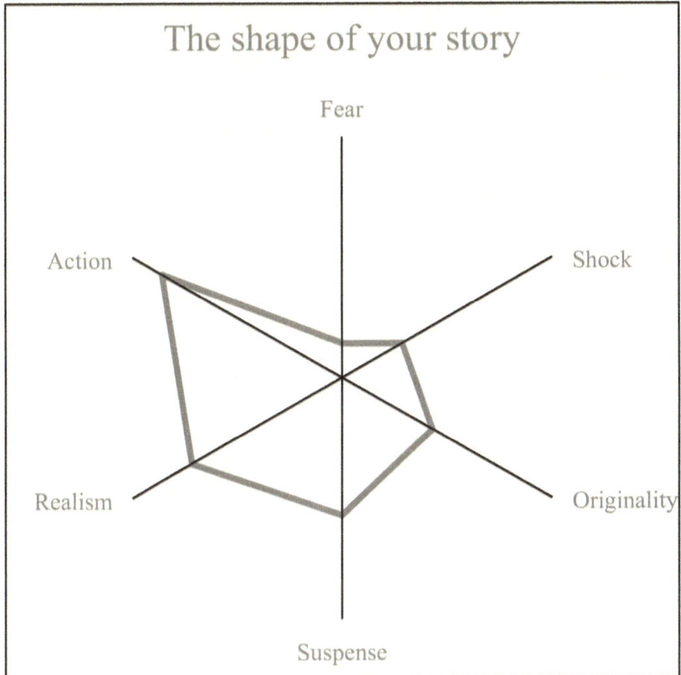

Plot outline:

Characters:

Character motives/what drives the story:

What makes this story unique to you:

46.   A travelling psychic refuses to work with your protagonist and her friends, and is eventually cornered and pressured into revealing they will all die in a week. This story could follow each team member individually as they cope with the news in their own way.

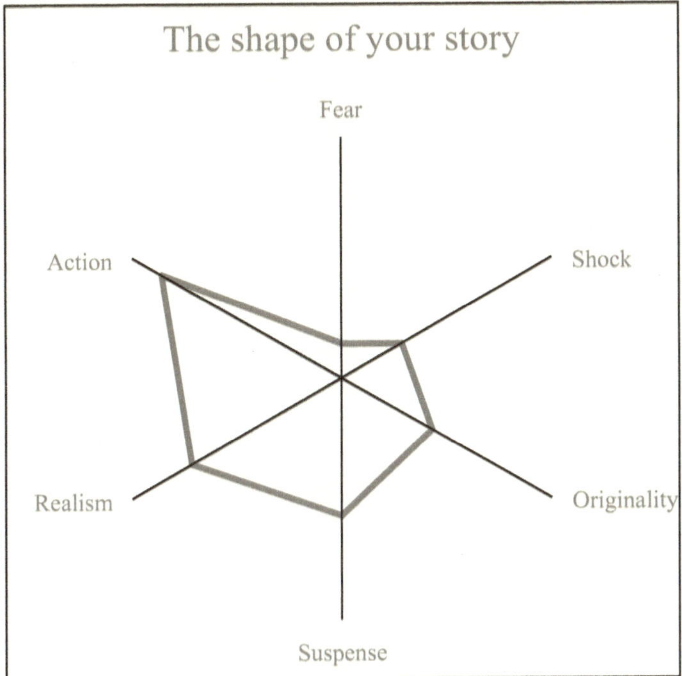

Plot outline:

Characters:

Character motives/what drives the story:

What makes this story unique to you:

47.　　　A 3-D printing company teams up with a brain reading company, inventing a machine that can create realistic 'golems' from your memories. Unfortunately, these horrific sculptures sometimes come to life.

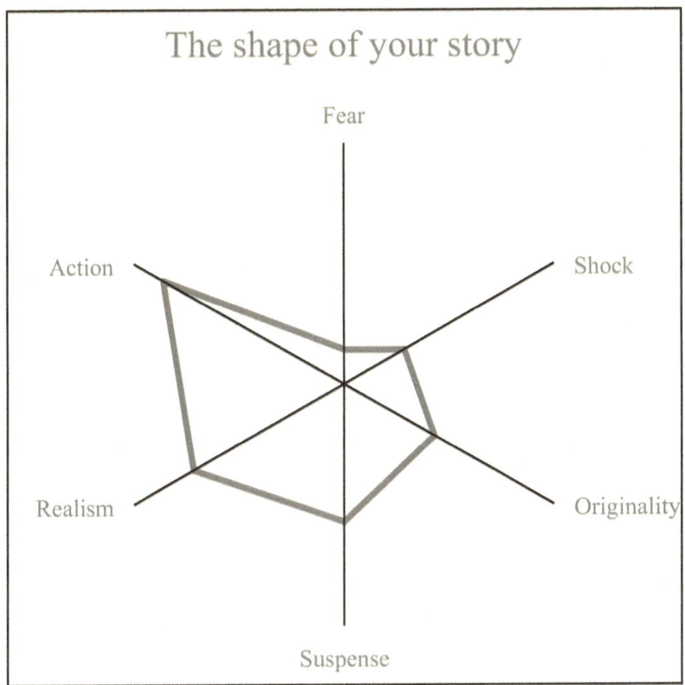

Plot outline:

Characters:

Character motives/what drives the story:

What makes this story unique to you:

48.　　　A wildlife photographer fakes his death in the woods in order to escape a debt. Weeks later he sees himself on TV, having returned to his town after finding his way back to civilisation. But this isn't him, it's a shapeshifting evil entity, and it's cleared his debts and started a promising career as a politician, obviously.

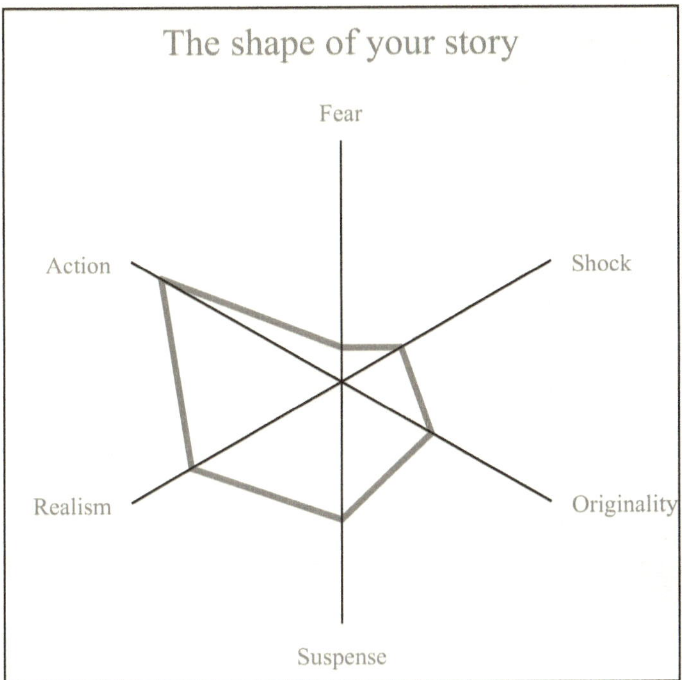

Plot outline:

Characters:

Character motives/what drives the story:

What makes this story unique to you:

Hello, just checking in. How is the writing going so far? How are you feeling about your progress?

Do you have a favourite prompt from the last four?

Do you have a favourite story, and if so, did that story come from your favourite prompt or another prompt? Why is it your favourite?

Have you written anything outside of your comfort zone recently? If so, how did this make you feel? Did you discover anything about yourself as a writer?

Is there anything you have struggled with recently?

Do you have any ideas for getting better at it?

What has inspired you today?

Optional tasks:

1. Use the space below to pitch a story that combines or borrows parts from the previous four stories. You could create a common theme between them, or invent recurring characters or locations.

2. Use the space below to write a short review of a chosen story from the perspective of a reader.

3. Identify one thing you are proud of from each story, and one thing you want to improve. Remember, these can be the same thing sometimes. You can still be proud of an action scene whilst wanting it to improve.

4. Invent your own prompt and share it with someone. If you don't know anyone, look online for writing groups. Remember to be safe, and if you have a really good idea for a story, keep it, it's your treasure.

5. Write a prequel for one of your stories that explains something about your characters.

49.   A planetary alignment causes a sudden shift in insect behaviour, resulting in swarms of insects attacking crowds of people, destroying crops and causing machinery to malfunction.

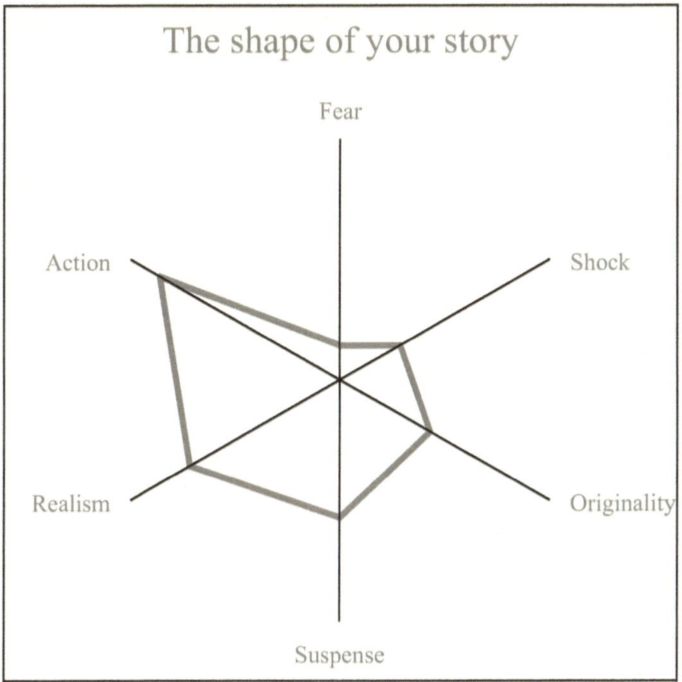

Plot outline:

Characters:

Character motives/what drives the story:

What makes this story unique to you:

50.   A fungus is discovered that eats human flesh, leaving only the brain behind, which it then assimilates into its growing mass. The resulting entity is trying to take over the world, one jungle explorer and uncontacted tribe at a time.

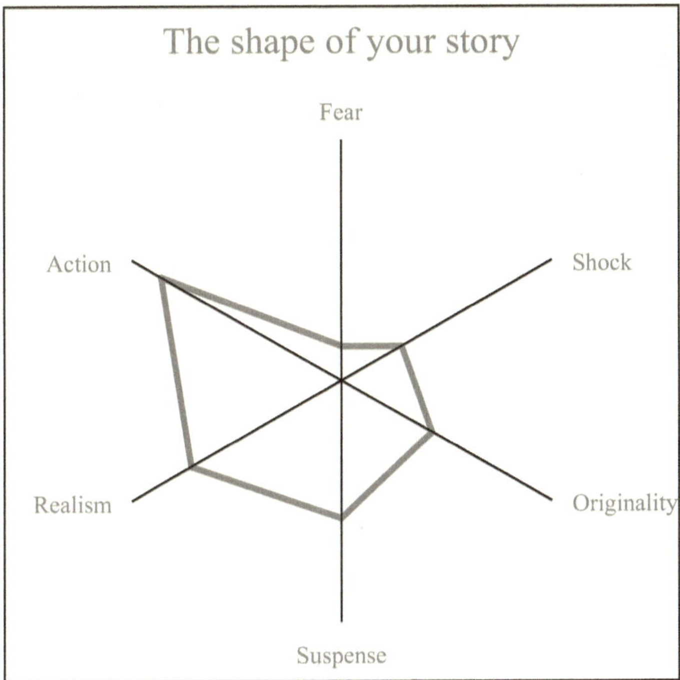

Plot outline:

Characters:

Character motives/what drives the story:

What makes this story unique to you:

51.   Whilst researching volcanic activity, a team of scientists stumbles upon a charred shrine at the base of an extinct volcano. Moving closer, they discover a blackened human skeleton standing upright, which then turns and attacks them.

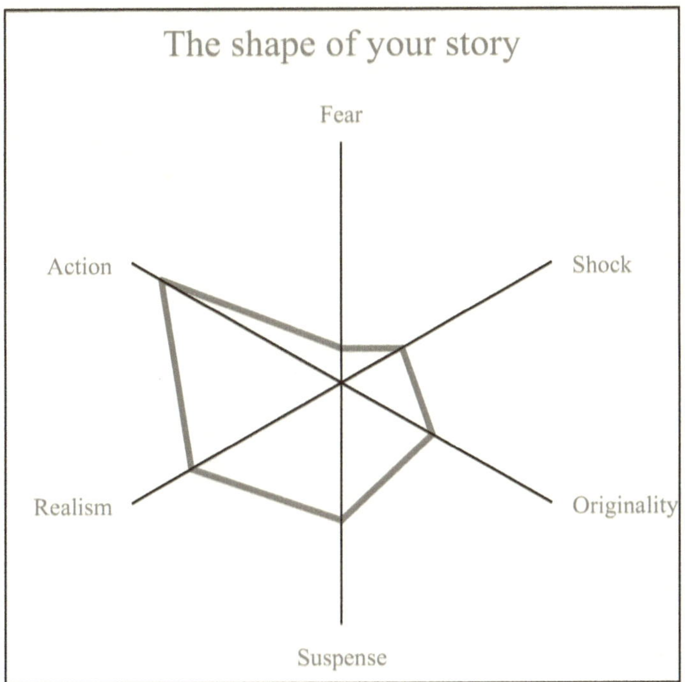

Plot outline:

Characters:

Character motives/what drives the story:

What makes this story unique to you:

52.   An oversized, robotically enhanced scorpion burrows its way out of a military base, heading for the nearest city.

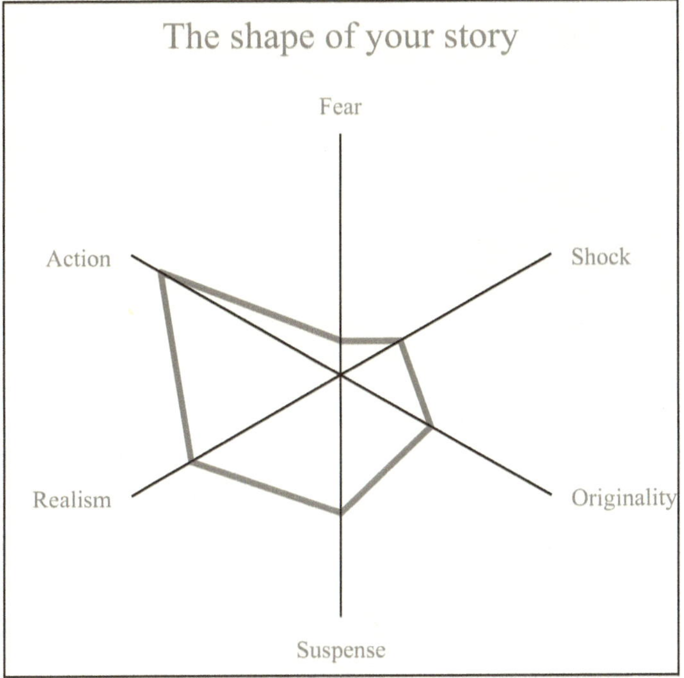

Plot outline:

Characters:

Character motives/what drives the story:

What makes this story unique to you:

Hello, just checking in. How is the writing going? How are you feeling about your progress? How did this year go?

Do you have a favourite prompt from the last four? How about from all of them?

Do you have a favourite story, and if so, did that story come from your favourite prompt or another prompt? Why is it your favourite?

Have you written anything outside of your comfort zone recently?
Did you discover anything about yourself as a writer?

Is there anything you have struggled with recently?

Do you have any ideas for getting better at it?

What has inspired you today?

Optional tasks:
1. Use the space below to pitch a story that combines or borrows parts from the previous four stories. You could create a common theme between them, or invent recurring characters or locations.

2. Use the space below to write a short review of a chosen story from the perspective of a reader.

3. Identify one thing you are proud of from each story, and one thing you want to improve. Remember, these can be the same thing sometimes. You can still be proud of an action scene whilst wanting it to improve.

4. Invent your own prompt and share it with someone. If you don't know anyone, look online for writing groups. Remember to be safe, and if you have a really good idea for a story, keep it, it's your treasure.

5. Sob uncontrollably as this book is almost over. Then take one of the last four stories and hide it from yourself. Try to rewrite it from memory in a few days, then compare the two and see what has changed (I use this method to rewrite novels sometimes, it makes them spicier).

So this is it. You've completed all 52 prompts in this book. But before you go, I have a few more questions I'd like you to answer to help your progress as a writer.

Are you a more confident writer now than you were 52 weeks ago?

Did you write any new prompts yourself?

Did you make any new friends, or have any brilliant ideas?

What was your favourite big idea?

What's your favourite prompt from this book?

What's your favourite story?

Which skills have you developed the most when working with this book?

Which skills would you like to continue working on?

Are there any genres you have written in that you wouldn't have written in otherwise?

Have you achieved your goals that we set out on the first few pages?

If not, that's okay. You might have changed your mind, or you might still be working at them. So, do you have any new goals, or are there new ways to get to your old goals?

End

And finally, this isn't a question. I wanted to thank you for purchasing this book and working through it. By doing so you have become your own tutor. You have discovered weaknesses and worked hard at improving them. By now you should know yourself better as a writer, know what you want to write and how you are going to write it. You should be proud of yourself. There are 52 great stories here because of you.

You have also helped Halfplanet Press become something big, and that means I get to make more of these books and help more people. So thanks for that too. Hopefully I'll see you in the next prompt book.

Halfplanet Press

134

www.ingramcontent.com/pod-product-compliance
Lightning Source LLC
Chambersburg PA
CBHW031255060726

47590CB00003B/912